Praise for

"This is a very touching book, a book full of pain and heartache, healing and restoration. This book will bless you if you or someone you love is struggling with sexual integrity."
STEPHEN ARTERBURN, Co-Author of *Every Man's Battle*

"I was captured by this book immediately. This is a challenging subject, and *The Shadow Christian* does it in a way that makes the message not only extremely relevant but fascinating to read."
SHAUNTI FELDHAHN, Author of *For Women Only*

"I was very moved by this book's honesty and constructive, not guilt-inducing, approach. In particular, I found the parable style to be very effective in helping one drop one's defenses. The reader starts out thinking that this is someone else's problem, then gets seduced into discovering that it is his also. There is no doubt that pornography is severely distorting the sexuality of good men, and that God is calling us to help men develop a sanctified sexuality. I believe that *The Shadow Christian* does just that."
DR. ARCHIBALD D. HART, Dean Emeritus
Fuller Theological Seminary School of Psychology

"*The Shadow Christian* tells the raw and honest reality of what happens when a man doesn't guard his heart and shares the long journey back. This book is a warning every man should read if he cares about his marriage, his family and his future."
BOB RECCORD, Founder and President
Total Life Impact Ministries

"Al & Linda's story is a message of the Gospel and redemption. This is the truth God's churches need to be sharing with men who are struggling with sexual temptation. I pray that others will discover the truths shared in this important book."

KIPPER TABB, Director, Celebrate Recovery/Marriage
Perimeter Church, Atlanta

"Wonderfully done. An excellent way for people to 'step inside' the healing process and understand it more 'experientially' than simply intellectually. A powerful testimony."

CHRISTOPHER MCCLUSKEY, Author of *When Two Become One: Enhancing Sexual Intimacy in Marriage*

"I honestly think that *The Shadow Christian* is the best material I have read addressing this subject. I was so encouraged by this story, which is shared with so much transparency and speaks truth regarding the complexity, depth and realities of sexual sin. Truly outstanding work!"

S. MICHAEL CRAVEN, Founding Director
Center for Christ and Culture

"A great little book. I highly recommend it for men and wives who have had this issue explode openly in their lives."

GEORGE OHLSCHLAGER, Executive Director, Int'l Board, American Association of Christian Counselors

"Masterfully uses the art of storytelling to open the eyes of men struggling with a universal problem."

NEW MAN Magazine

"Although the focus is on sexual addiction, *The Shadow Christian* is a primer on the process of repentance on our walk of maturity in Christ. A great choice for small group study."
REV. MARK A. DERBY, District Superintendent
Baltimore-Washington Conference, UMC

"Al and Linda Cole have written an incredible book, and I've read a lot of books on sexual purity and on addiction. This is a human story that is absolutely wonderful."
RICK SCHATZ, Former President and CEO, National Coalition for the Protection of Children & Families

"This book will pierce the hearts of men who truly seek to walk the path of sexual integrity. It transcends race, age, and social boundaries in tackling one of today's most troubling issues. I highly recommend it."
TONY J. GATEWOOD, College Campus Minister
InterVarsity Christian Fellowship/USA

The Shadow Christian

A Parable about Sex, Love,
and the Grace of God

By Al and Linda Cole

"But he said to me, 'My grace is sufficient for you,
For power is made perfect in weakness.'
So I will boast all the more gladly of my weaknesses,
So that the power of Christ may dwell in me."
—2 Corinthians 12:9

"Pornography is the sum total of the written and visual material that is trivial, cheap, and nasty and is meant to titillate. It is sexual stimulation without reference to beauty, personal relationship or love. It is a distortion of all that truly belongs to authentic sexuality."

–Michael J. Taylor,
from *Sex: Thoughts for Contemporary Christians*

This is the true story of a Man and a Woman. Chances are you know a couple like them.

The
Shadow
Christian

1

"Nothing is covered up that will not be uncovered,
And nothing secret that will not become known."
—Luke 12:2

It had been a day like any other for the Man, but his picture-perfect marriage was about to collapse. When he reached the top of the stairs, the Woman was waiting for him, holding up a single sheet of paper.

"Does this look familiar?" she asked, angrily.

The blood drained from his face. He was staring at a list of pornographic Web sites. The Woman had caught him—again. The first time, the Man had told her he had only done it twice, which was a lie, and promised never to do it again. But over the past year his habit had gotten worse.

"How often do you do this?" the Woman demanded. She was hurt and confused. The Man could not tell her the truth.

"Just once in a while," he said, unconvincingly.

The Woman asked again, "How often?" The Man labored to come up with an answer she would accept.

"Almost every day," he said, afraid to be totally honest.

It was more than the Woman wanted to hear.

"How could you do this?" she asked, her voice trembling.

The Man tried to defend himself and said, "Maybe if we had sex more often, I wouldn't have needed to." He knew his words were unfair.

"You can't blame me for this!" the Woman shouted. Her mind was racing. All she knew for sure right now was that she couldn't live with a man who couldn't live without pornography. She wanted to grab a heavy object and throw it at the Man. Instead, she handed him an article she had printed out.

The Man cringed when he saw the title "Sexual Addiction" in large type. He went through a list of questions: Yes, he had taken risks to look at porn. Yes, he had been spending more and more time with it. Yes, he had tried to stop on many occasions. The questions progressed to phone sex, prostitution, extra-marital affairs, and more. The Man was ashamed to have the Woman see him this way. He put down the article and looked up at her.

"Why is this happening?" the Woman asked. She desperately wanted to understand. The Man shook his head. He didn't have a good answer for her or for himself. They argued for a long time, and afterwards the Man agreed to sleep in the extra room.

When he crawled into bed, he pulled the covers over his head, hoping to hide from the unpleasant reality that Internet pornography had taken over his life. For the past two years, he had regularly visited porn sites at work, putting his job, his reputation, and his family's security in jeopardy. He had stayed up late at night and gotten up early in the morning to look at porn. He had looked at porn whenever the Woman left the house. He had told himself that what he was doing was harmless. But deep down he had known that each time he did it he was betraying his wife, separating himself from God, and chipping away at his character. He had prayed for the strength to stop, but he kept going back to it.

The Man awoke at 4:30 a.m. and began to read the Bible. He was looking for some sign that God could forgive him. He stopped when he came to this passage:

> *"Just so, I tell you, there will be more joy in heaven over one sinner who repents than*

over ninety-nine righteous persons who need no repentance." (Luke 15:7)

Before he drifted back to sleep, the Man understood three things:

God had already forgiven him.

His wife might not.

His life would never be the same.

2

"Wretched man that I am!
Who will rescue me from this body of death?"
—Romans 7:24

The Man couldn't face the Woman today. Last night, she had forced him to look in the mirror, and he didn't like what he saw: a man who had risked his marriage, his family, and his soul for make-believe sex with nameless strangers.

As he drove away from the house, he attempted to reconcile his pornography obsession with the rest of his life. He loved his wife. He was a good father. He went to church every Sunday. He was active in ministry. He was successful in his career, well respected and well liked.

So why was he drawn to pornography?

Hadn't he been introduced to sex like most boys of his generation, through the photos in *Playboy* magazine? He had ogled women as far back as he could remember. Wasn't that his entitlement as a red-blooded American male? Wasn't it natural that he would eventually be lured by the Internet, which offered unlimited variety and complete anonymity? To justify his preoccupation with sex, the Man had told himself throughout most of his adult life that he probably had a stronger than average libido. Today, it sounded like a pitiful excuse.

At sunset, the Man headed home. What could he say to the Woman? That he was sorry? He had been sorry a year ago, but he had continued to betray her. The Man entered the house and went into the extra bedroom. He sat in the dark and began to cry. After a few minutes, the Woman came to the door.

"Where did you go today?" she asked, with no emotion in her voice.

"I just drove around," the Man said. "I needed some time to think."

"I did a lot of thinking too," the Woman said.

The Man was silent.

"I'm not going to live with this," she stated, calmly.

The Man knew the Woman well enough to know that she meant it.

"How could you do this to us?" she asked. The question hung in the air for a while, and then the Woman left the room.

The next morning, the Man reluctantly called about a Workshop he had heard about on a Christian radio station. It was hard for the Man to admit to the person at the other end of the line that he struggled with pornography. The voice on the phone said there would be a Workshop next month in a nearby city. The voice also said he could recommend counselors who specialized in sexual addiction. The Man felt as if he were acting out a scene in someone else's life.

At four o'clock the Woman left to go shopping because the Son was coming home from college for the weekend. Ordinarily, the Man would have headed straight for the computer and lost himself in a fantasy world of porn images. But he was too shaken to go anywhere near the computer. At dinner, for the sake of the Son, the Man and the Woman pretended that nothing was wrong.

Later that evening, the family watched a PG-13 video that contained a brief scene with several young women in bikinis. The scene was not overtly sexual, but it was provocative enough to make the Man uncomfortable and send the Woman out of the room in a huff. The Man followed her downstairs.

"I guess you're enjoying yourself," she said, crossly. The Man tried to change the subject.

"I don't think the movie's very funny," he said.

The Woman glared at him.

"How do I know what you're thinking when you look at things like that?" she asked.

The Man sensed that this was a question that would linger in the Woman's mind for a long time. Why shouldn't it? Hadn't he given her the impression that he was too weak to resist any sexual temptation? He wondered if they would ever be comfortable watching TV together again.

In the midst of that thought, the Woman asked, "Why haven't you opened the e-mail we got about the Workshop?"

"I just haven't been ready to look at it yet," the Man said.

"You don't want to face this," the Woman said, pressing him.

No, I don't, thought the Man, but he said, "I'll look at it tomorrow."

They exchanged harsh words for a long time, until there was nothing left to say. The Man went to his room and opened his journal. He needed to wrap himself in a happy memory of the way things once were. He began to write:

> *If I could pick one scene from our life together to live out through eternity, it would be the time we kissed on your sofa. It was the most tender and intimate expression of our love, you and I lost in each other's arms. Maybe I loved you at first sight, but kissing you that night was the first expression of that love. From the moment we met, you filled my heart with feelings I didn't know I could feel. All I wanted to do that night was hold you forever and look into your eyes. Once we kissed, I wanted to kiss you forever. I would do anything to recapture that closeness.*

He wondered if they would ever feel that way about each other again.

The next morning, the Man started to cry when he read the e-mail about the sexual purity Workshop. The comments of people who had attended gave him hope, but a part of him didn't want to admit that he needed help. He simply wanted all of this to go away. Finally, he got up and walked into the kitchen.

"What did the e-mail say?" the Woman asked.

"I think I should go," the Man said, solemnly. "I need help."

"I think you should go, too," the Woman said. She saw that the Man's eyes were red, and she wanted to comfort him. But something held her back. They had faced many challenges in their years of marriage and had always been able to draw on each other's strength. This was different. They were at war with each other, even as they were trying to survive as a couple.

For the next two weeks, the Man and the Woman went about the business of living as best they could, but anxiety was never far below the surface. By Thanksgiving evening, the charade was wearing thin, and the Woman accused the Man of having an affair.

"I've never been unfaithful to you," the Man responded.

"What you've done on the Internet is the same thing," the Woman shot back. "Doesn't the Bible say that if a man lusts in his heart, he is committing adultery? In your mind you've had sex with lots of women."

The Man tried to assure her that he had never been with another woman, but she only got angrier. The Woman knew that the Man routinely lied about little things to avoid looking bad. Why would he admit to having an affair when their marriage was hanging by a thread?

"What about our friends?" the Woman asked, growing more agitated. "Have you ever lusted after any of their wives?"

The Man said nothing.

The Woman was voicing all the doubts she had harbored over the years, as well as new doubts the Man had put in her mind. She had reached her breaking point.

"Our marriage is *over!*" she said through gritted teeth. Her words and the hatred on her face cut like a knife. The Man could see no love left in her eyes, only the pain of betrayal. How could she ever trust him again? The Man felt a profound emptiness, as if the Woman's trust were a living organism that had been ripped from deep inside of him.

The battle of words escalated, and the Woman began to hit the Man on his chest and arms. He pushed her away, but she kept coming back, each time with increasing fury. In frustration, the Man shoved her and she fell to the floor. It felt like the end of the world to both of them. The Woman got up and left the room, and the Man silently prepared for bed. He prayed for sleep to come quickly.

The Man awoke during the night with a gnawing in his stomach. The beautiful girl he fell in love with was in more pain than he could ever have imagined himself causing her. He asked God to ease her suffering. Then he prayed, "Please, God, have mercy. Please, God, help us."

It was morning, and sunlight filled the room. The Man was curled up under the covers, praying, "God have mercy on us. Please help us." The Workshop was two weeks away, and the Man wondered if he and the Woman would still be together then. After last night, he was only sure of one thing:

He needed a miracle.

3

"Therefore confess your sins to one another,
And pray for one another, so that you may be healed."
—James 5:16

T he Man sat on a bunk in a room with cinder block walls. A wooden writing desk and chair separated two single beds. It felt like a prison cell, and the Man felt like a criminal. A half hour ago when he registered for the Workshop, he was certain that the young lady behind the counter could see into his soul and discern his deepest, darkest secrets. She couldn't, of course.

The Roommate arrived just before he and the Man had to leave for orientation. They exchanged introductions and walked together to the meeting room. When they got there, the Man saw a group of men ranging in age from about twenty to late sixties. He was relieved that none of them had a scarlet letter on his forehead.

As a counselor led the group in song, the Man realized that these men were no strangers to Christian music. Some were singing harmony while others were holding their arms outstretched. These were good men who had stumbled, he thought, men who, like him, were seeking hope and healing. When the singing was done, the Leader walked to the podium and read from Scripture:

> *"Be glad about this, even though it may now be necessary for you to be sad for a while because of the many kinds of trials you suffer. Their purpose is to prove that your faith is genuine. Even gold, which can be destroyed, is tested by fire; and so your faith,*

*which is much more precious than gold, must
also be tested, so that it may endure. Then
you will receive praise and glory and honor
on the Day when Jesus Christ is revealed."
(I Peter 1:6-7, TEV)*

The Man began to relax, sensing that God had brought him here to help him.

"No one should expect a miraculous overnight transformation," the Leader declared. "God will equip each man to manage his problem one day at a time."

Then the Leader told his story. He was sexually abused as a child and pursued physical love in various forms, attempting to recreate the feeling that someone found him lovable. In his late teens, he accepted Jesus as his Savior and eventually became a minister. But because he never was able to confess his desires to anyone, he continued to seek love in unhealthy ways—affairs, prostitutes, swinging—until a Christian therapist gave him an opportunity to disclose his sexual sins and longings.

Throughout his testimony, the Leader described himself as a "sex addict," similar to an alcoholic in recovery who is one drink away from a relapse.

The Man didn't like the label. He had read that viewing pornography caused the brain to release chemicals that could be as addictive as alcohol, cocaine, or even heroin. But was this truly an addiction? The question would have to wait. When the session was over, he approached the Leader and extended his hand.

"Thank you for sharing your story," the Man said. He could see that the Leader was emotionally spent.

"It's tough every time," the Leader said, shaking the Man's hand.

As the Man and the Roommate got ready for bed, they talked about why they were here. The Roommate said he agreed to come simply to placate his wife. Then he sat down at the desk, opened his laptop computer, put on headphones, and started to play a video game.

The Man read the Bible for a while then rolled over and stared at the wall. The first small group session was tomorrow, and he was not eager to share his secret with anyone. But he was here, and he would do whatever was necessary.

With the Man gone, the Woman felt a sense of freedom. It was the first time in a month that she could take a deep breath and try to absorb what was happening. She had wanted the Man out of the house and out of her life. She was finally going to have some peace. She wanted to forget about pornography and the damage it was doing to them and to millions of other families.

The morning lesson dealt with the nature of sexual sin. The more the Man learned, the worse he felt. He had tried to tell himself he was a victim of his sexual desires, but today he could not deny that each time he had fantasized about women—whether they were walking down the street, in magazines, on television, or on the Internet—he had made a deliberate choice. He had dishonored his wife and rebelled against God. One verse the Leader read stayed with him:

> *"Very truly, I tell you, unless a grain of wheat falls into the earth and dies, it remains just a single grain; but if it dies, it bears much fruit." (John 12:24)*

The Man knew his old way of life had to die.

When it was time for him to tell his story to the small group, the Man spoke from his heart. The men were sympathetic. They had been there. They understood. His group

27

included an 18-year-old, a man in his twenties, two about thirty, one in his fifties, and the Roommate.

One of the 30-year-olds said his wife left him a year ago when she discovered that he was heavily involved with Internet porn, phone sex, and prostitutes. He still loved her and wished that someday she could forgive him. He came to the Workshop because he believed he still had value in God's eyes.

The teenager spoke next. He had been addicted to Internet porn for three years, and his mother had caught him several times. When she caught him again a few months ago, he agreed to get help. The Man admired the boy for taking steps to address his addiction, but it forced him to consider how easily the Son could fall into the same trap. It was the last thing the Man wanted to think about right now.

The Man was glad to have a chance to talk with other men who were struggling to come to grips with the consequences of sexual sin, but he was having a hard time getting past his feelings of self-hatred. He didn't believe he deserved another chance. Several times today, he had pictured the Woman's face and had seen the pain written there. He couldn't bear the thought of how deeply he had hurt her. How could he ever make things right?

Whether or not he could save his marriage, the Man knew he had to make things right with God. He had managed to stay away from pornography for a month, which encouraged him. With God's help, he told himself, he could change. The prospect of returning to his secret life was too horrible to contemplate. But why would God help him when he had fought God at every turn? The Man read one of the day's Scripture verses:

> *"Yet there is one ray of hope: his compassion never ends. It is only the Lord's mercies that have kept us from complete destruction.*

Great is his faithfulness; his lovingkindness begins afresh each day. My soul claims the Lord as my inheritance; therefore I will hope in him." (Lamentations 3:21-24, LB)

At that moment the Man realized that out of love for him, God had exposed his sin and forced him to deal with it.

During the second small group session, the Man asked a question that had been bothering him: Was this really an addiction? The Counselor said that they approached compulsive sexual behavior as an addiction so no one would underestimate how difficult recovery would be. Fair enough, the Man thought. But he still wasn't comfortable with the label.

When the Man told the group that he hadn't felt worthy of his wife's love for a long time, the Counselor responded with compassion.

"How could you when you were keeping this secret?" he asked.

The Man knew he had been a fool. Instead of trying to become the man the Woman deserved, the man God had created him to be, he had disappeared into a world of make-believe.

At the end of the day, the Roommate was as guarded as he had been in the group, but the Man sensed that something had changed. Just before lights out, the Roommate put on a gospel CD and began to type a letter to his wife. The Man opened his journal and wrote two things:

God's compassion never ends.

Sexual sin is a choice.

4

"Those who love me I will deliver;
I will protect those who know my name.
When they call to me, I will answer them;
I will be with them in trouble,
I will rescue them and honor them."
—Psalm 91:14-15

"True repentance," declared the Leader, "means we must be willing to look closely at the damage our behavior has caused."

No problem, the Man thought to himself. *I've been doing that for weeks.*

The Leader went on, "Your behavior has shaken your loved one's confidence and taken away her sense of safety." The Man closed his eyes and imagined the Woman, alone in their house, looking sad, lost, and scared.

"She is having doubts about herself," the Leader said. "She is feeling stupid for ever trusting you, and she's having to ask herself, 'Why would God give me a man in marriage who would break my heart?'"

The question brought the Man to the brink of tears.

The assault continued, "You have shattered her trust." The Leader seemed to be talking directly to the Man. "You have insulted her and made her feel neglected. You have delivered a permanent blow to your marriage that will leave a scar, even if it does eventually heal."

Enough! the Man wanted to shout. But he just sat there and listened.

"You will never be able to fully understand the pain

you've caused," the Leader insisted.

When the session finally ended, the Man was numb.

He decided to call the Woman and try to ease her pain. When she answered the phone, he started to cry. He wanted to tell her how sorry he was, but he could barely get the words out between sobs. He was a penitent man who had realized only a few minutes ago how terribly he had hurt his wife. But all that came through the phone was a desperate apology that sounded inadequate even to him.

When the Woman spoke, the Man could hear anger in her voice. She had had a day and a half alone to think and search for answers. She told him she had been reading about sexual addiction, and some of what she had read seemed to say that men were helpless victims of sexual temptation, which made her furious. She had also read that men usually try to blame their wives. She guaranteed him that she was not going to let him make her feel guilty or doubt herself.

She hated the thought that many women accepted those false accusations and—instead of taking a firm stand—decided that they were the ones who needed to make changes to keep their husbands from sin. She remembered finding a "girlie" magazine under some blankets in the closet in a spare bedroom at her parents' house when she was in her early twenties. It was the bedroom where her dad took his daily afternoon nap. Her mother had chosen to look the other way. The Woman was determined not to make the same mistake.

The Man tried to assure the Woman that the Workshop was about men taking full responsibility for their actions. But how could he provide her any relief? He was the enemy. He had broken his vows and lied repeatedly to cover his tracks. In her eyes, he was a drowning man who would say whatever was necessary to save himself.

The Woman could hear sincerity in the Man's voice, but she was too angry to offer him any solace. She couldn't stop thinking about how he had deceived her. When she hung up the phone, she didn't know what to believe.

As she replayed the phone call in her mind, she recalled being touched by something the Man had said. A week ago, she had told him that through all the tough times they had endured together, the one thing she had always been able to count on was their relationship. She had heard the Man choke back tears when he said how sorry he was that he had taken that away from her. The Woman had never seen the Man display such sensitivity, and she was thankful for whatever it was that had forced these emotions out of him.

The Man was frustrated at how the conversation had gone, but he was glad he had called. The Woman had needed to vent some of the anger she had bottled up over the past couple of days. He headed for his small group, emotionally drained and was content to listen to the other men's troubles. The 18-year-old was especially hard on himself today. He was experiencing overwhelming guilt and couldn't bear the thought of being who he was. The Man was feeling the same thing.

"Our sins are separate from us," the Counselor said to the teenager. "They do not define who we are."

It was an important distinction for the Man. He had done bad things, but that didn't make him a bad person. After this morning's brutal lecture and his conversation with the Woman, the Man needed all the reassurance he could get.

The Woman spent the day looking for evidence of an affair. She wanted to know how far the Man's sexual obsession had gone. She pored over months of phone bills and credit card statements. She couldn't believe she was at a place in her marriage where she felt this was necessary.

Whenever she came across anything suspicious, her heart pounded and her hands shook. She hated the Man for putting her through this. She didn't know whether she wanted to discover something incriminating so she could end the nightmare and start a new life, or whether she hoped she wouldn't find anything, even though this wouldn't eliminate her nagging doubts.

She checked out some unfamiliar phone numbers and found nothing improper. But she still wasn't satisfied. What if he had been with a prostitute and had paid in cash? As exhausting as the day had been, the Woman knew she was facing another sleepless night.

At the end of the evening session, the Man went back to his room and thought about what he had learned. He could reduce his exposure to sexual temptation, but he wasn't going to be able to avoid it completely. Good-looking women were still going to cross his path when he was walking down the street minding his own business. Or sexy beer commercials were going to pop up while he was watching a ball game on TV (The Leader called this "getting slimed")

To deal with these situations, the Man was instructed to train his eyes to quickly look away from the source of temptation and not dwell on it, so that attraction, which was normal, would not progress to unhealthy desire. Over time, healthy habits would replace sinful ones. It made sense, but the Man wondered if someone who had given in to sexual temptation his whole life could change his ways. He knew the Woman was wondering the same thing.

The Man looked over at the Roommate, who was sitting at the writing desk, quietly typing on his computer. A gospel CD played in the background.

"Another letter to your wife?" the Man asked. The Roommate nodded.

"I've been doing a lot of thinking," he said, taking his hands off the keyboard. The Roommate stood up, walked over to his bed, and sat down. He folded his hands and looked

34

up at the Man. The Roommate's face was drawn. Something got to him today, the Man thought. The Roommate was feeling the weight of it all and needed to talk.

"When I came here, I figured my wife would get over this," the Roommate said, softly. "Now I see how much I've hurt her. I love my wife, and I want to make things right with her and with God. I called her tonight and told her so."

The Man mostly listened over the next half hour. He was glad the Roommate finally was being honest with himself. The Roommate understood that making things right was going to take considerable time and effort on his part. When the Roommate finished talking, he returned to the desk to finish his letter.

The Man looked over his notes. One sentence stood out: *Without honesty, intimacy is impossible.* The Man had wanted closeness, but he had been unwilling to let the Woman know him. He had wanted her to see him not as he was, but as he thought he ought to be—so he lied, even about small things. He underlined verse 13 in Psalm 139: *"You created every part of me; you put me together in my mother's womb." (TEV)* The Man could accept that a loving God had created him, but he still couldn't accept that he was worthy of God's love, or the Woman's love, or the love of his children.

He thought about something the Leader had said this afternoon: God had brought the Man to his knees, just as He had brought St. Paul to his knees on the road to Damascus, to prepare him for greater things.

"When we are helpless," the Leader had declared, "we are more vulnerable, more pliable, and therefore more likely to move toward God."

The Man was willing to admit that he needed God and that he would need the Woman's patience as he worked through this. But did he have any right to ask her for anything?

The Woman was not ready for the Man to come home tomorrow. She wondered how she could have been so clueless about her husband's Jekyll and Hyde behavior. How could she have been so blind? Last night, when she read all the cards the Man had given her over the years, she noticed that many of them contained an apology about something and a promise to do better. Did the Man have a conscience after all? Was he actually feeling guilt at the same time that he was writing such tender and loving words to her? Who was this man she married? The Woman wasn't sure she wanted to find out.

The Man couldn't sleep. It was 2 a.m. and he was overcome with remorse. He had betrayed his wife. He had broken his vows. He had shattered her trust. He silently cried out to God with the words of a Bible passage he had scribbled down this afternoon:

"Heal me, for my body is sick, and I am upset and disturbed. My mind is filled with apprehension and with gloom. Oh, restore me soon. Come, O Lord, and make me well. In your kindness, save me. For if I die, I cannot give you glory by praising you before my friends." (Psalm 6:2-5, LB)

On this final morning of the Workshop, the Man wasn't anxious to leave. He had felt safe here, surrounded by people who accepted him as he was, who wanted to help him. They had embraced him as a repentant sinner. He didn't know what awaited him at home.

Just then, the Leader walked up to the podium.

"We began this journey," he said, "just as the apostle Peter began his, with many misconceptions about ourselves. Like Peter, we failed Jesus and thought we had separated ourselves from Him forever."

The Leader related how Jesus had shown Peter the fullness of His love, even after Peter had denied Jesus three times. The Man understood what the Leader was saying: Even though the Man had failed his wife and had sinned again and again, God had never stopped loving him. The Man felt tears form in his eyes.

At the end of the session, the men gathered up their gear as they exchanged goodbyes. Many were embracing; some were crying. The Man assumed that they were asking themselves the same question he was: What now?

The Man dropped off his key and said a few more goodbyes—to the 18-year-old from his group, to a couple of men with whom he had shared a meal or two, and to one of the counselors. When the Man reached the parking lot, the Roommate was there waiting. They agreed to meet once a week to hold each other accountable for their behavior as they tried to rebuild their lives.

As the Man drove through the gates of the retreat center and back into the real world, three thoughts occupied his mind:

God uncovered his sin out of love for him.

He would never fully know the Woman's pain.

Intimacy without honesty is impossible.

5

"We are afflicted in every way, but not crushed;
Perplexed, but not driven to despair; persecuted,
But not forsaken; struck down, but not destroyed."
—2 Corinthians 4:8-9

The Man pulled his car into the driveway, turned off the engine, and sat in silence. When he entered the house, the Woman met him in the hall and they hugged for a long time, as if they hadn't seen each other for months. She sensed that he was on the verge of breaking down.

When the Son walked into the room, the Man embraced him and thought about the 18-year-old at the Workshop. The Man didn't ever want the Son to go through what that boy had gone through. After a while, the Man led the Woman out to the porch so they could talk in private.

As they sat facing each other, the Man took the Woman's hands in his and looked into her eyes.

"I want to be completely honest with you for the first time in our marriage," he said. Tears ran down his cheeks, but he made no attempt to hide them. He didn't try to compose himself, as he normally would have done.

The Woman had never seen him like this.

"I want to tell you the truth about everything," the Man said. "The counselors told us to confront our wives right away and disclose anything we had kept from you."

The Woman studied his face and braced for the worst.

"I did look at pornography at work," the Man admitted. He had denied this for weeks. "I did it every day. I don't know how I could have been so stupid." The Man felt an immediate sense of relief, but the Woman was stunned.

She suddenly realized that his obsession had gotten so bad that he had been willing to risk his job—and their financial security—because of it. She sat motionless, waiting for a bombshell to drop—an affair, or multiple affairs, or maybe something worse. What would she do when she finally heard the words?

The Man tried to reassure her that he had nothing left to reveal, that he had never had an affair. He desperately wanted her to believe him, but he could see the doubt in her eyes. He wanted her to know that he was different now. There was so much he wanted to say, but he was so full of emotion that he feared he wasn't making much sense.

It didn't matter to the Woman. She just wanted the Man to talk. She had wanted him to talk from the heart for such a long time.

Eventually, the Man read her a list of changes he was going to make. The list included joining a support group, seeing a Christian therapist once a week for at least six months, installing a filter to block access to pornographic Web sites, finding an Accountability Partner, reading the Bible at least five minutes a day, and more. The Man made a commitment to the Woman and to God to carry out these changes. He also made a pledge to remain sexually sober, which meant he would avoid any form of sexual stimulation other than his wife.

After an hour or so, they went back into the house. It had been an emotional reunion, and there would be time to talk more tomorrow. For now, the Man was happy to be home, to lie in his own bed next to his wife, and to have hope.

The next day, the Man tried to convey to the Woman what the Workshop had been like and how it had affected him. The Man felt as if God had performed a root canal on his soul.

But the Woman could not see into his heart. She could

not know the loneliness he had felt because of his sin, the moments of deep despair, or the closeness he had experienced with God while he was away. The Man had heard preachers use the phrase "personal relationship with Jesus Christ," but he had never understood what it meant. He had felt nearer to God these past few days than at any other time in his life.

The Woman wanted to believe the Man had changed, but she was afraid.

Looking back over their recent past, she could see that she had often sensed that something was bothering the Man.

Whenever she had asked him about it, he had insisted that nothing was wrong. When his mood wouldn't change and he wouldn't open up to her, she got upset that he couldn't trust her with his inner thoughts, and they had often ended up arguing.

When the Woman thought about how much the Man had held inside, she realized what release it must have been for him to open up to the other men at the Workshop. Typically, the Man would do or say almost anything rather than admit a mistake. The Woman knew it must have been difficult for him to tell his story, and she recognized that it was a step he had needed to take.

Over the next few days, there were glimpses of the kind of intimacy the Man and the Woman had longed for. One night, the Woman invited the Man to dance in their living room. He held her in his arms, and they looked lovingly into each other's eyes as they moved slowly across the floor. For an hour or so, they were new to each other again. It was as if all the barriers between them had vanished and all the hurt had been washed away.

But the wound was deep, and doubt and fear continued to haunt them.

The next morning, the Woman was angry, raising questions the Man could not answer: Could any man fall into this trap, or was there something about the Man that made him more susceptible? Was this really an addiction? And if so, did that mean there would always be a possibility that he could relapse? The Woman was not sure what they were dealing with, and neither was the Man.

Every morning for the next few weeks, the Man played his guitar and sang the songs he had sung at the Workshop, trying to hold on to the emotional high. He prayed that God would help him find positive outlets for the energy he had been wasting on sexual sin, and he bought a small gold cross to wear on a chain to remind him that God was near to his heart. He also met twice with his Accountability Partner.

The Man sought God each day by studying the lives of great men of Scripture, such as King David, and found that even the most blessed of men had disappointed God. David had done terrible things and yet God had forgiven him and continued to use him to accomplish great things. David had also paid a price for disobeying God, and so had he.

The Man continued to write in his journal, and prayed and read the Bible every morning. This morning, he came across a passage that spoke to him:

> *"He found them wandering through the desert, a desolate, wind-swept wilderness. He protected them and cared for them, as he would protect himself. Like an eagle teaching its young to fly, catching them on its spreading wings."(Deuteronomy 32:10-11, TEV)*

The Woman often thought about the sincerity the Man had displayed the night he came home from the Workshop. It helped her forget about the pain for a while. The Woman thanked God for the positive changes in the Man. But she wondered if they would last.

At times, the Man became discouraged. Making all the

changes he had promised was proving to be difficult. He lived in a small town and was having no luck finding a support group.

When he reluctantly called Sexaholics Anonymous, a recorded message asked him to describe what he was looking for and to leave his number—someone would call him back. He felt as if he belonged to a secret society, and he didn't like the feeling. He wondered if it would be easier if he were an alcoholic. At least it would be socially acceptable. But a *sexaholic*? It sounded depraved. *I don't want this to be my life*, he thought.

The Man was embarrassed about having to reveal his secret to the Pastor, but he knew it a necessary step. It was another opportunity to get his sin out of the darkness and into the light. The Pastor had never counseled anyone who was struggling with sexual addiction, but he was understanding and supportive. They agreed to meet for an hour a month over the next six months.

The Pastor was a good listener, with a relaxed and earnest manner that was soothing. The Man told the Pastor some of what he had learned at the Workshop, such as identifying situations that increased his likelihood of committing sexual sin. The Man told the Pastor that one regular source of temptation was the magazine rack at the supermarket. Now that the Man was aware that this was a problem area, he could make a conscious decision to avoid that part of the store.

The Pastor was glad the Man had confided in him, and he thought the changes the Man had promised to make were good ones. They ended the hour by praying together. When the Pastor had gone, the Man remembered a line he heard on the radio: *A church is supposed to be a hospital for sinners, not a museum for saints.*

The emotional swings were sudden and unexpected. Last night, the Man and the Woman were laughing and making small talk, and a few minutes later, he saw her glaring at him.

"What's wrong?" he asked.

Silence.

He asked again, "What's the matter?"

"Why haven't you found a therapist yet?" she finally responded.

"You know I've been looking," he said.

"If it was important to you," she said, "you would have found one." She was furious that he had not taken care of this, and she was beginning to doubt that the changes he had made were genuine.

"Do you think I'm trying to fool you?" the Man asked, indignantly.

"It wouldn't be the first time," the Woman shot back.

The Man saw the hatred in her eyes. He had hoped that time and prayer would heal the wound, but not enough time had passed.

Her questions kept coming: What about all the sexual images he had stored in his head over the years? Wouldn't they keep popping up? The Man admitted that this still happened, but now he blocked them out by multiplying large numbers in his head, which worked surprisingly well. But he knew it must have sounded ridiculous to the Woman.

———————————

There were days when the Man did not want to relive the pain they were going through by writing about it in his journal. But he had made a promise to God, to the Woman, and to himself, and if he failed at this simple task, it would only make him feel worse.

The Woman frequently thought about a separation. She

was unable to go a day without having doubts about the Man. She wanted to sign a contract with God promising that her faith would grow if only He would erase the memory of these last few months. She knew that adversity was supposed to make you stronger, but she didn't want to be stronger. She just wanted the pain to stop.

As the days passed, the Man tried to reassure the Woman that he was different.

One afternoon, he thought he was being sensitive when he offered to go to the store with her rather than stay home and create doubt in her mind about what he might do if he were left alone. Instead, she accused him of going with her because he couldn't trust himself. It hurt to be wrongly accused, and it hurt worse to know he was causing the Woman pain. But how could he complain when he had lied to her so many times? It had only been a month since the Man had returned from the Workshop, full of hope, and yet it seemed so long ago. He took comfort in one thing:

In spite of everything, God still loves you.

6

"Trust in the Lord with all your heart
And do not rely on your own insight.
In all your ways acknowledge Him,
And he will make straight your paths."
—Proverbs 3:5-6

On the way to his first appointment, the Man wasn't sure he needed to see the Therapist for six months. But he had promised the Woman. As he drove, he contemplated the state of his soul. He didn't know if his marriage would survive, but he knew that if he were to die right now he would go to Heaven. For the moment, the Man was at peace.

At the Workshop, the Leader had said that men struggling with sexual sin didn't need to know the roots of their problem to stop the behavior.

He had been right.

The Man had not looked at pornography since the night the Woman confronted him more than two months ago.

But now the Man needed to understand how it had become so important to him—and so did the Woman.

He had read some early research on sexual addiction, which found that the vast majority of sexual addicts had suffered some form of physical, sexual, or emotional abuse in their lives. The Man's grandmother had repeatedly told him he was no good when he was a child, and he wondered if this had had any lasting impact on him.

More recent studies indicated that there were now millions of people who were having problems with sexual compulsion who never would have had them if the Internet had not come along—viewing pornography repeatedly could release chemicals in the brain that were as addictive as heroin. He didn't know what to think.

The Therapist was about the same age as the Man and dealt with sexual issues from a Christian perspective. After a few minutes, the Man sensed that he had found someone who could help him. The Man recounted the events that had led him here, described the Workshop, and described where he and the Woman were in their relationship and in their lives.

The Therapist interrupted the Man when he said the words "my problem."

"What problem is that?" the Therapist asked, knowing full well what the Man was talking about.

"My problem with pornography," the Man responded. *There. I said it. Are you happy now?*

"What exactly is your problem with pornography?" the Therapist insisted. He called the Man on this every time.

The Man felt like a third-grader who was being prodded by his teacher. Eventually, he got the point. He was avoiding saying that he had been obsessed with visiting pornographic Web sites, so he had substituted "my problem" because it didn't sound as harsh. The Therapist was telling him that words mattered: Before the Man could be honest with the Therapist, he would have to be honest with himself. Fair enough, the Man thought.

The Man disclosed that he had struggled with a poor self-image for most of his life. Now that his sin had been exposed, it was even worse. He recalled a joke from a Woody Allen movie, "Don't knock masturbation. It's sex with someone I love." For the Man, the exact opposite was true. Each time he had "acted out" this way, he had hated himself more.

As they were wrapping up, the Man casually mentioned that since he had cut off his intake of sexual images, he didn't get aroused as often.

"Of course not," the Therapist said. "You aren't fueling your lust anymore."

The Man felt stupid for bringing it up.

The Therapist suggested that the Man list his good qualities and accomplishments for next time. He also asked the Man to think about how his parents and close family related to him and to each other when he was a child and write down early sexual cues.

After the session, the Man stopped at a nearby restaurant to meet the Roommate, who had agreed to be his Accountability Partner.

Their plan was to get together once a week to talk about their ups and downs on the road to recovery. Today the Roommate seemed distant and reserved, and the conversation was formal and unsatisfying. The openness he had exhibited toward the end of the Workshop had vanished. They agreed to meet again next week, but the Man headed home feeling frustrated with how the encounter had gone.

Later that night, the Man worked on his assignment for the Therapist, but he could not come up with anything good to say about himself. The weight of his sin was crushing him. In his mind, whatever good he had done was now buried beneath a mountain of failure. Although the Woman often tried to assure the Man that she still loved him, he felt he didn't deserve her love.

The Woman came over and sat down next to him. She picked up his notebook and began to make a list of his achievements. The Man was touched by her kindness.

The Man was annoyed at having to write about his childhood,

but he forced himself to do it. One thing jumped out at him: his parents and close relatives were a lot like the TV families of the 1950s, where the husbands and wives expressed polite affection for each other with no hint of sexuality. He also recalled that most of the husbands were passive.

"What I saw was women controlling men," the Man said at his next session.

The Therapist leaned back in his chair and urged the Man to continue.

"Do I resent that the Woman controls how often we have sex?" the Man asked.

The Therapist said nothing. He seemed content to listen, and the Man wondered if they were accomplishing anything.

When the session was over, he still didn't know why sex had become so important to him. The Man was annoyed. Once again, he had bared his soul, and once again he had little to show for it. On the way home, he thought about what he would say to the Woman, who was expecting him to come back with some solid insights about his "problem."

The Woman had already arrived at some conclusions of her own. Now that she knew the Man had been looking at pornography on the Internet, she understood why his interest in having sex had increased over the past couple of years. It also explained why he had resisted praying with her at bedtime.

Over the next few weeks, there was so much animosity between the Man and the Woman that the Man could hardly breathe. He had decided to stop seeing the Roommate because their subsequent meetings had been as unsatisfying as their first. The Man felt that the Roommate was not ready to be honest with himself or with him.

The Man had also given up on finding a group within three hours of where he lived. The Woman was concerned about the Man's failure to keep these commitments, but she also knew he had tried his best. She was satisfied that he was still seeing the Pastor once a month and the Therapist once a week.

In the middle of one session, the Man brought up his tendency to lie to avoid looking bad.

"Sex addicts are good liars," the Therapist said matter-of-factly. "They have to be."

The Man didn't like hearing it, but he knew it was true.

The Therapist listened intently as the Man talked about his longstanding desire to be in control of things, even as he recounted the ways his life had been tragically out of control for a long time. Through it all, one question gnawed at the Man: How would the Woman ever feel comfortable having sex—or making love—with him again? He had equated sex with love for so long that he still believed that his recovery hinged on working things out in the bedroom.

"When I try to show the Woman love and tenderness now, she thinks I'm only doing it as a way to initiate sex," the Man complained.

"Haven't you trained her that way?" the Therapist asked.

The question stung the Man.

"I guess I have," he answered, contritely. The Man had to acknowledge that part of him expected—or at least hoped—that there would be a sexual payoff for his recent displays of kindness and affection. He wanted to love his wife unselfishly, but he could see that he wasn't there yet and that the Woman had good reason to doubt him.

"How can we ever put all this behind us?" the Man asked, weary of the struggle.

"You can't," the Therapist said. "You'll have to work through it."

It sounded like a pop psychology cliché, but the Man understood: He couldn't change the past, but he also couldn't ignore it. Bad things had happened, and he and the Woman would need to recognize how those things were still affecting them before they could ever build a healthy relationship.

Seemingly out of nowhere, the Therapist asked, "What if the two of you committed to a period of abstinence?"

The Man thought he was joking.

How could not having sex for two or three weeks be a good thing? But as they talked, he realized that taking sex out of the picture for a while might help the Woman to see that the Man's attentiveness was authentic. It would also prevent him from harboring any ideas of sexual reward for his actions.

"The Woman said the other night that she has often felt used, and that I've seen her simply as a body to satisfy my needs," the Man said.

"Can you blame her?" the Therapist asked.

The Man was ashamed. It hurt him to know he had made the Woman feel that way. Later that night, he and the Woman agreed to abstain from sex for two weeks.

The Woman welcomed the chance to remove sex from the equation. Whenever she had heard someone on Christian radio talk about how God wanted married couples to enjoy a healthy sex life and that wives were supposed to surrender themselves, she had wanted to scream. Under the circumstances, how could she feel comfortable being the "dutiful wife"? What about her self-respect? How could she be expected to be intimate with her husband when the thought of sex elicited such anger and hurt?

Meanwhile, the Man was slowly coming to realize one thing:

Sexual sin is a misguided search for intimacy.

7

"For if you live according to the flesh,
You will die; but if by the Spirit
You put to death the deeds of the
Body, you will live."
—Romans 8:13

The Man could hardly wait to see the Therapist this afternoon. Two weeks had passed, and the Man hoped that abstaining from sex had convinced the Woman that he could be attentive without having an ulterior motive.

He had been counting the days, which he realized was an indication that he was still preoccupied with sex. But he brushed aside that concern. To the Man, sex equaled love. No sex meant no love, and he badly needed love these days.

The Therapist and the Man had covered a lot of ground over the past months, and the Man felt good whenever they were together. The Therapist was compassionate, but he didn't tolerate bullshit, which the Man assumed the Therapist heard frequently in his line of work.

The Woman was coming with the Man to see the Therapist for the first time. He had invited her before, but she had not been ready. She had joked that it was his head that needed to be examined, not hers.

The Woman was apprehensive. She didn't know what to expect. Ever since she had learned about the Man's betrayal, she had not been able to cry, and this was unusual. Anyone close to her knew she was an emotional person. TV commercials, movies, happy times, sad times—her kids could predict the exact moment to look at her and see tears streaming down her face. She was afraid she might break down in the Therapist's office. She could picture herself sobbing uncontrollably.

The Therapist greeted the Man and the Woman in the waiting area and led them to a room down the hall. The three of them sat opposite each other like the points of a triangle. The Woman sensed that the Man was uncomfortable with her there. The Man was anxious about how the session would go, but he was glad the Woman had come.

The Therapist turned first to the Man.

"How do you think you've changed?" he asked,

"I'm a lot better about letting my feelings out," the Man said proudly. He looked over at the Woman, expecting her to sing his praises.

"What do *you* see?" the Therapist asked the Woman.

She hesitated for a few seconds.

"Maybe he's a *little* bit more open about his feelings," she said, trying to be charitable, "but not like he was when he came back from the Workshop."

The Man couldn't believe his ears. He was *much* more loving, open, and honest. Couldn't she see that?

"What do you think about what the Woman just said?" the Therapist asked, as if he had anticipated her response.

"I'm not happy about it," the Man replied. "I thought the changes I've made were more noticeable. Maybe I'm not as open as I was after the Workshop—I mean, I was on an emotional high—but am I really only slightly better than I used to be?"

The Man became defensive.

"I know how closed up and private I used to be," he insisted, "and I know I'm much more open now."

The Woman and the Therapist stared at him as if he were too dumb to grasp the obvious.

"How would I know how much you were keeping from me all these years?" the Woman asked. All she knew was that the Man had built a wall between them and would not let her in.

The Man took a moment to absorb what she said.

"I guess I still have a long way to go," he said softly.

The Therapist turned to the Woman.

"If you knew the Man had an affair," he asked, "would you feel much different than you do now, knowing all the times he had used pornography?"

The Man panicked.

"Just so you know," he assured her, "I didn't tell him I had an affair."

The Woman flashed back to a TV show she had seen the other day about men who had had affairs. As the wives were discussing their shock and pain, the Woman realized she had experienced much of what they were describing. After a few seconds, she responded to the Therapist's question.

"I don't think I would feel any different," she said. "I feel that the Man has had numerous affairs with these unnamed women on the computer, and I definitely feel he has been unfaithful to me."

The Man was uneasy about the question, but he understood why the Therapist had asked it. He wanted the Man to see that looking at pornography on the Internet was just as hurtful to the Woman as an affair.

Finally, the Therapist moved on to the subject of abstinence. The Man and the Woman had agreed to take sex off the table for the past two weeks, and both of them were uneasy about what would happen next.

"How are we supposed to feel comfortable about sex now?" the Man asked.

The Woman was wondering the same thing.

The Therapist looked at the Woman and then at the Man.

"You're not," he said. He then told them they had more work to do, so the Man and the Woman decided to extend the period of abstinence indefinitely.

Looking back over the years, the Man could see how often he had thought about having sex with the Woman and how frustrated and angry he had gotten whenever they didn't. He realized that his actions had put more distance between them, and he was embarrassed at how desperate he had been for love, which he automatically linked with sex. He wanted to do whatever it would take to repair their relationship, even if it meant no sex for a while.

A few nights later, the Woman offered the Man a glass of wine.

"Do you want to fool around?" she asked.

At that moment, there was nothing on earth the Man wanted more.

"Is this a trick question?" he joked, trying to put them both at ease. Then he placed his hand on her shoulder and kissed her lightly on the lips.

"I don't think it's a good idea," he heard himself whisper. "I don't want to do anything that would make us feel bad tomorrow."

He was glad the Woman wanted to be with him, but he knew it was more important to honor his commitment to abstain. He was beginning to see that rebuilding trust was the issue, not sex. Could she trust him? Could he trust himself? As much as he thought he needed sex, he said no in the hope that one day they might enjoy each other fully and without doubts.

Over the weeks that followed, the Man began to treat the Woman differently. He would softly touch her face and tell her how beautiful she was. In the morning, he would cuddle with her and gently stroke her hair. He saw that his obsession with sex had robbed them of this kind of closeness. The Man remembered that the Woman was a precious gift from

God, and he realized he had treated her badly. He had learned an important lesson:

Love doesn't demand its own way.

8

"For I will restore health to you,
And your wounds I will heal, says the Lord."
—Jeremiah 30:17

Tears came easily to the Man now. He had held so many tears inside for so long, trying to be strong when his heart was swollen with hurt. It was as if the poison he had allowed to enter his soul over a lifetime was slowly working its way out of him.

"I cry all the time," he told the Therapist one afternoon. "I cry when I think of all the hurt the Woman is feeling. I cry when I look at pictures of my kids. I cry for no reason sometimes. I can't seem to focus at work, and I have no enthusiasm for anything."

The Therapist was not surprised. "It sounds like you're experiencing grief symptoms," he said.

"Grief?" The Man was incredulous. "About what?"

"You're grieving the loss of your old way of life," the Therapist replied.

"What are you talking about?" the Man asked. "I'm glad I abandoned pornography."

"Yes, but sexually acting out was something you could count on to dull the pain and relieve stress," the Therapist explained. "And now it's gone."

The Therapist told the Man that he also was grieving over all the time he had lost to sexual sin, time of closeness with his wife and kids, time apart from God, time he couldn't get back. During this period of grieving, the Therapist said, other unresolved issues might surface.

The Man related an incident from last week. He was going through a drawer full of photos and greeting cards from old friends and came across a large get-well card the sixth grade class had sent when the Son was seriously ill. Even though the Son had since made a complete recovery, the Man wept uncontrollably as soon as he read the card.

"It was as if all the fear I had held in when he was sick was coming out," the Man said.

The Therapist nodded. He waited for the Man to speak next.

Finally, the Man said, "I've felt for a long time that I never grieved properly over my mother's death. I moved away right after she died."

"Perhaps you should write her a letter," the Therapist suggested.

That night the Man sat down with his journal:

Dear Mom,

I miss you so much. I'm writing because I need to let go of some feelings I've carried with me since you died. I barely shed a tear at your funeral. Instead, I chose to comfort others because your death came as such a shock to them. The Woman and I are facing a difficult period in our marriage, and I'm trying to understand some things about myself. One of them is that I've carried some unresolved anger toward you for allowing me to suffer abuse as a child. Maybe you did all you could. I just feel the need to forgive you. Somewhere along the way, I learned to guard my heart and not let anyone in. In fact, the reason I'm feeling so much pain these days is that I am finally learning how to open my heart. I truly wish your grandchildren

*could have had you around a lot longer. We
all miss you and love you.*

The Man felt no need to cry. He had accepted her death and
her life as it was.

The Man knew he needed to let his emotions out to heal, but
the Woman often acted as if he had no right to feel the way
he did. How could he tell her he was sad or confused when
she didn't want him to be sad or confused? But if he didn't
admit that he sometimes felt lost, he would come across to
her as guarded.

It had been so freeing when the Man had been able to
open up to the Woman after the Workshop. She hadn't
judged him then. She had simply listened. The Man was
aware that he had wrapped many protective layers around
himself, and he knew it would take time to peel them away.
He felt as if the Woman wanted to take a hot poker and burn
through them all at once.

One evening, they decided to try an exercise the
Therapist had recommended to help them feel more
comfortable about sharing their feelings without fear of
being reproached. One of them would make a statement and
the other would try to repeat it as accurately as possible. The
purpose was to force the listener to concentrate on what was
being said rather than think about a response.

The Man and the Woman quickly discovered how difficult it was to truly listen to each other. They soon fell back
into their familiar pattern of only half listening, and their
conversation quickly escalated into an argument in which all
their pent-up anger and frustration came out.

The Man felt as if he were going to explode. Their world
was collapsing and he could do nothing to prevent it.

63

Finally, in frustration, the Woman blurted out, "After all our years together, I don't really know you."

It was unnerving for the Man to hear her say it, but the truth was that he didn't know himself. He had uncovered a lot in recent months: He resented women because of his grandmother's constant badgering; he harbored animosity toward his mother and father for being afraid to stand up to her; he used sex—in reality and in fantasy—to control women and avoid rejection; he resented the Woman when she withheld sex, which he equated with love. He wasn't anxious to learn more.

A few days later, the Man complained to the Therapist, "All I get from the Woman is criticism. I don't feel I'm getting any love from her."

The Therapist rocked back in his chair.

"Can you think of any ways that she does show you love?" he asked.

The Man thought a moment and then looked at the Woman.

"She's here," he said. "I guess that's one way."

The Therapist paused to let the words sink in.

The Man knew he had broken the Woman's heart, and yet she was sitting here beside him. She had refused to accept his sinful behavior and had forced him to confront it, which was another expression of love. The Man thanked God for the Woman. He could see that she was a model for other women in this situation. He had learned an important truth:

True love endures hardship.

9

*"I praise you, for I am fearfully and wonderfully made.
Wonderful are your works; that I know very well."*
—Psalm 139: 14

The Man did not give the Woman a present for Mother's Day—not even a card. She said he did it to prove to himself that he was a bad person. When the Man mentioned this at his session, the Therapist agreed with the Woman.

"The child who thinks he's no good does not want to let go of the image he has held on to for so long," he said. "Whenever you begin to change that image, he becomes uncomfortable and tries to sabotage what you're doing." The Therapist suggested that the Man conduct an interview with himself as a child.

It sounded like a silly idea to the Man. He had always made fun of people on daytime TV whenever they cried about childhood issues. *Get over it!* he'd shout at the screen. But as he thought about it on the way home, he recognized that the Therapist was right about one thing: The Man had been feeling better about himself. He had begun to believe that God had created him with unique talents and intended good things for him. Yet something had prevented him from honoring the Woman on Mother's Day.

Later that evening, the Woman dug up a photograph of the Man at age nine in a baseball uniform, holding a bat on his shoulder. The Man tucked it in his notebook and walked out to the porch. As he looked at the old photo, he tried to imagine what that boy was thinking:

—*I don't like to see my mother cry.*

Q. Why is she crying?

—*She's crying because of me. My grandmother says mean things about me.*

Q. What does your grandmother say?

—*She says I'm no good. She says it a lot.*

Q. Where is your dad?

—*He hardly ever says anything to my grandmother. My mom gets mad at him if he does. Then they fight with each other.*

Q. Does this happen a lot?

—*Yes, and it's getting worse.*

Q. Why is it getting worse?

—*My grandmother said it was my fault that my brother fell out of a window.*

Q. How was it your fault?

—*She said that my whining called up the devil. She said my parents would have to beat me to get rid of the devil.*

Q. How did that make you feel?

—*I was scared my brother was going to die.*

Q. What else would she say?

—*When she really got mad, she would say, "He'll be hanging from the gallows at 13."*

Q. Did your parents ever say anything to your grandmother?

—*My mom would tell her not to say it, and then my mom would cry.*

Q. Do you believe what your grandmother said?

—*I don't know.*

The Man came back into the house.

"How did it go?" the Woman asked. She always encouraged the Man to do whatever the Therapist suggested, hoping for some kind of breakthrough that would wrap everything in a neat package.

"It's the first time I've actually felt the pain I felt as a child," the Man said. Whenever he had thought about his grandmother, it had been a vague memory. "I guess I've avoided going deeper because I didn't want to feel the pain again." The Therapist had said that the Man needed to feel the hurt so he could accept that what had happened was real. Once he accepted that it was real, he could forgive his grandmother.

The next morning, the Man opened his journal and wrote a letter:

> *Dear Grandma:*
>
> *I don't know if I ever hated you when you said horrible things to me. You were my grandmother, and I loved you. I don't think I understood then how cruel your words were. But you did. You must have been hurt terribly in your life to be able to hurt your grandson, and your daughter, that way. I hope my mother was able to forgive you before you died. I am still struggling to fully comprehend how your unkind words invaded my life, threatened my marriage, and made me feel so worthless that I turned to pornography to escape my self-loathing. But pornography only made those feelings worse. I have spent years hating myself for what you did to me. All that matters now is that I know you were wrong about me. I forgive you, Grandma. Rest in peace.*

The Son and the Daughter were home for the summer, and they quickly noticed the tension in the house. The Man and the Woman had been able to disguise their feelings when their children had visited on breaks and weekends. As hard as it had been to live together over the past seven months, the Man and the Woman had been able to express their anger and frustration openly. Now, they could not conceal the sad fact that their marriage was in crisis. They wanted to be honest with their children—they needed to know what was happening—but the Man wasn't ready yet.

It seemed to the Man that he could never say anything right these days. Or if what he said was right, he was saying it at the wrong time. The Woman often cut him off in mid-sentence and was highly critical, even in front of the children. When he brought this to her attention, she admitted she sometimes took out her hurt and anger toward him this way. Yet she continued to do it.

The Man was reluctant to challenge the Woman because he felt his past sins had diminished his moral authority. He worried that the children would think that the Woman was controlling or that he was afraid to stand up to her. He suddenly realized they were acting like his parents.

At daybreak the Man was curled up on the sofa in the fetal position. He remembered that Jesus said we must be as little children to enter the Kingdom of Heaven. It felt good to be a child this morning, to be dependent on God rather than having to be responsible for everything.

The next afternoon, the Man told the Therapist that he was frustrated and angry that God wasn't providing clearer direction.

After a long silence, the Therapist said, "Maybe you're too focused on what He wants you to do instead of how He wants you to be with Him."

The Man told the Therapist how much he wanted to feel the intimate connection with God that he had felt in the days and weeks after his sin was uncovered.

"Why do you think you felt so close to God then?" the Therapist asked.

Without hesitation, the Man replied, "Because He was all I had."

"God still is all you have," the Therapist said, leaning forward in his chair. "But the good news is that God is all you need."

The Man thought about this for a while and realized that he had sought God desperately in those dark days and that he needed to seek God just as passionately now.

A few days later, the Man made a selfless gesture, with no thought of payback, sexual or otherwise. He presented the Woman with a kitten for her birthday. She had hinted for weeks, but he had feared it would add to his stress. Despite his reservations, he got the kitten because he knew it would make her happy, and she needed some joy in her life.

The Man had not anticipated that the kitten would immediately take to him and regularly crawl up his chest and nuzzle his face. He wondered if the kitten sensed that he was more capable of love now. The Man thanked God for opening his heart and realized:

God is a loving father.

10

"We also boast in our sufferings,
Knowing that suffering produces endurance,
And endurance produces character,
And character produces hope."
—Romans 5:3-4

O n their last night of vacation, the Man and the Woman went to dinner. They were holding hands across the table and enjoying a beautiful sunset when two provocatively dressed women sat directly in the Man's line of sight. It made the Man and the Woman uncomfortable, but neither of them said anything about it.

The Woman could not shake the memories of how the Man used to check out every female he saw. She had observed how some men could stay focused on what they were doing, even after spotting an attractive woman in a revealing outfit. She wondered what made them so different from the Man, who always had to take a longer look.

It seemed as if every time she came close to opening her heart to the Man, something like this would happen to bring back the nagging doubts. She had trusted him before, and she had gotten hurt. She didn't want to be hurt again.

On the way to the car, the Woman couldn't contain her frustration.

"You must have noticed those women," she said.

The Man braced himself and considered a response.

"Yes," he said, cautiously.

"Why didn't you switch seats with me so you wouldn't be facing them?" she asked.

"I didn't want to bring it up because I didn't want you to think I couldn't control myself," the Man said.

It was the truth, but it didn't satisfy the Woman. They argued about it for the remainder of the night.

Later, as he sat alone in the dark, the Man recalled the time the Woman described their arguing as a "setback" at one of their sessions.

"How is it a setback" the Therapist had asked, raising his eyebrows. "You dealt with the problem, and now you know how to deal with that situation in the future." He reminded them that they had communicated their needs and fears to each other and insisted, "That is a sign of growth."

The Man supposed that the Therapist was right. They were growing, but growing was painful.

In the morning, the Man watched the Woman make breakfast and remembered falling in love with her smile. When the Woman smiled, everything seemed good and right. She had not been smiling much these days. Tears began to form in his eyes. He was so afraid of losing her that he couldn't think straight. He could not give her what she needed right now—safety, security, hope that would endure for more than a day or two.

He looked out the window and saw people on the street laughing and seemingly carefree. They had problems, too. But somehow they were able to experience joy for at least a little while. There was so little joy now for the Man and the Woman. He was desperate for her love, and he was suffocating her. He was the Man, and he was supposed to be strong. Instead, he was a lost child, hoping his heavenly father would reveal the next chapter of their lives.

He walked outside and stood in the sun for a while. Sweat trickled down his arms, and in the calm he thought of one of his favorite lines from Scripture: *Be still, and know that I am God!" (Psalm 46:10)* He closed his eyes and asked God to speak to him. A cooling breeze blew across his skin. It felt as if God were whispering, "Yes, my child, I am here."

The Man tried to recall past vacations with the family, but those memories of laughter and love were shrouded in a haze that rendered them more distant than they really were, as if they belonged to another family. He remembered a photo of the Woman wearing a swimsuit and walking toward him, smiling. She had loved him so much then.

The Man knew he had nothing to be ashamed of these days except the past, which he couldn't change. He had expelled the demon that had possessed him, and he prayed that God would heal their marriage. If there was anything good to come from last night's quarrel, it was that the Man could separate himself from his former sins. He was sorry the Woman was upset, but he didn't feel worthless anymore. He smiled and thought to himself:

God will not abandon me.

Growth is often painful.

11

"If we say that we have no sin,
We deceive ourselves,
And the truth is not in us."
—1 John 1:8

R evealing weakness had always been hard for the Man. But the time had come for him to tell the Son and the Daughter that he had used pornography off and on for most of his life. What would he have thought about such a revelation from his father? How could his children understand when he didn't fully understand it himself? What would they think of him? After dinner, he mustered the courage to read them these words:

> *You know that your mother and I have been having problems. You also know that I've been meeting with a Christian counselor for the past six months. I've been seeing him because I've had a problem with pornography for a long time. I have been putting off telling you because I was afraid you would stop loving me, and I could not bear that thought. I want to be honest with you about what this has done to me and to your mother.*
> *It started with a natural curiosity about girls and sex, but that natural curiosity gradually became an unhealthy and destructive habit that I thought about almost obsessively at times. I told myself it was harmless, but I*

knew it was wrong. The prospect of losing your mother brought me to my senses and got me to seek help. Last year, I attended a Workshop with dozens of other men who wanted to be free of this curse. One member of my group was an 18-year-old boy who had been struggling with pornography for three years. I should have talked with you about this as soon as I got back, but I was ashamed. I apologize for that.

I want you to know that pornography is a terrible evil that destroys lives. It damages the people who view it and hurts those who love them. My use of pornography made it impossible for me to have an honest relationship with God, and it shattered the world your mother and I were living in. It nearly consumed the good and loving person God created me to be, and it has taken your mother and me to the brink of divorce. It is only through the grace of God that I was able to quit, which I did eight months ago. We're trying to rebuild our relationship, and I pray every day that we will. I'm being honest with you because I love you and want to protect you.

I want to share some of the insights I've gained about some incidents from my past, how they have affected me, and how my behavior has affected my relationship with your mother and with you. I have tried for a long time to hide my feelings and project an image of having it all together, even when I felt afraid, confused, and lacked self-confidence. I have lied or put up a false front so people would not see my flaws. I have been afraid for most of my life that if people saw me as I truly was, they wouldn't accept me.

I now know that these feelings originated in my childhood, when my grandmother would regularly tell me that I was worthless. As a result, I have sought love and acceptance while deep down I didn't think I deserved it. A voice inside kept repeating what I had heard so often as a child: You're no good. Although I have accomplished a lot in my life and have a loving wife and wonderful children, I remained emotionally distant because I continued to believe I was unlovable. This belief made me more susceptible to the lure of pornography, which holds out the promise of intimacy without the risk of rejection.

I have guarded my heart for so long that it is very hard for me to open it—but that is what I'm trying to do because I want to feel the fullness of your love. I have tried to hide my feelings, and it has almost cost me my marriage. Because I have not been completely honest with your mother, I have lost years of closeness we could have had with each other. I'm telling you this because I want you to be able to build healthy relationships in your own lives. I want you to be able to admit when you fail, and I'm sorry if I've made it hard for you to say, "I messed up." We all mess up sometimes. I've learned that it's okay to be scared, or confused, or sad, or angry, or whatever it is that you feel. Those emotions are real and they must be allowed to come out. I want our family to be about loving each other as we are and asking for help when we need it.

Don't ever consider pornography to be harmless entertainment for yourself or for the people you associate with. It is wrong in God's eyes, and I know first-hand the pain it can cause. I hope that by baring my soul to you, it will free you to open yourselves up to me and to others. I don't want you to make the mistakes I've made.

When the Man was finished, the Son and the Daughter hugged him. He was glad he had told them, and he was relieved. A week later, he visited the Older Son, who lived in another state, and delivered the same message. He had learned a valuable lesson:

It takes courage to admit weakness.

12

*"Do not remember the former things,
or consider the things of old.
I am about to do a new thing; now it springs forth,
do you not perceive it?"*
—Isaiah 43: 18-19

More than a year had passed, and the Man and the Woman were still together. There had been glimmers of hope that they could rebuild their marriage, but they quickly were snuffed out by old fears and doubts.

The Man had made it hard for the Woman to love him. His face and his manner displayed the sadness that often engulfed him. He was brooding and cross, smiling only occasionally to fight back tears. His heart was growing cold, even as it should have been giving out warmth to his family. He had withdrawn again. He still prayed to God each day for help, but he doubted that God would help him. He didn't understand why God was allowing him to sink lower.

Church had become an island of refuge for the Man and the Woman. Being around other Christians was a ready source of energy and inspiration. As a way to thank God for blessing them in so many ways—and as a way to turn their thoughts to something positive—they spent most of their free time doing volunteer work.

In the midst of one project, a church friend put his hand on the Man's shoulder and smiled. He could not have known how much that simple gesture meant to the Man, who was feeling very low that particular day. The Man saw it as yet another sign of God's grace.

As they went through their days, the Man and the Woman wondered if things would ever be right between them again. Their marriage had been shattered into a million pieces. Even if they could somehow put the pieces back together, why would they want to when their relationship wasn't what it should have been?

The Woman often felt that their entire marriage had been a fraud, but the Man knew they had shared much genuine love. He recognized that his secret life had prevented them from having the kind of marriage God intended, but he didn't believe it rendered everything else meaningless.

One day, the Son asked the Man if going to counseling was helping. The Son was home on break and had heard his parents arguing the night before. The Man had to shake his head and laugh because he often asked himself the same question. The best answer he could come up with was that without counseling, he and the Woman would have separated long ago.

The Woman decided not to come with the Man to today's session. Instead, she handed him a note to take with him. When he sat down with the Therapist, he read her words out loud:

> *The Man has become paralyzed. He rarely seems happy. He says he is seeking God, but he recently admitted being angry with God. I believe he is in a state of depression, and I feel we must address it. I've been thinking that he may need medication to help him pull out of his depression. I don't know much about it, but I feel we need to try this*

approach. I don't know how to help him anymore. I am extremely frustrated and often feel I am doing more harm than good. I am running out of patience, and it is hurting both of us.

The Therapist suggested trying an anxiety medication, and the Man reluctantly agreed. He was disappointed that he could not cope without pills, but he knew he needed something to pull him out of his despair. He thought back to the night his sin was uncovered. He had had no idea of the hell he and the Woman would have to endure.

That night the Man stood on his driveway and looked up at the heavens. He had never seen such a starry sky. And he had never felt so alone. He was holding on to a simple belief that God was shaping him and the Woman through this ordeal for a larger mission, but he sometimes wondered if this was a form of conceit. He often imagined that God laughed at his confusion. "If only you will trust me," God seemed to say, "there will be contentment."

At 2 a.m. the Older Son called the house, crying. He was confused about his life and said he had always had trouble expressing his feelings. The Man told him that his tears were flowing freely because of years of pent-up emotion. The Man should know. The Older Son had not learned to share his feelings from watching his dad, a typical pretend-to-have-it-all-together male. The Man told him that everything would be okay and suggested that he find a quiet place to pray and ask what God wanted him to learn from his pain. The Man had been asking God the same question.

In the morning, the Man watched one of the cats play with its tail. He knew that when the Woman awoke, she would talk to the cats and they would know she loved them. She had so much love inside, love she found easy to give. He had love inside, too, love that could cover her in roses and make her smile like she did when she was a little girl. But it didn't flow out as effortlessly as hers. He wished it did.

As the Man walked out to the mailbox, he looked at the gray sky, which matched his mood. He wished he could close his eyes and wake up in new surroundings. They would be moving in a few months and he hoped better days were ahead.

He picked a letter from the stack of mail and opened it. The Workshop organizers were inviting him to an alumni weekend at the end of the month a few hours' drive from his home. They also were inviting alumni to share their stories with the men who would be attending the Workshop for the first time, men who would be where he had been fifteen months ago. He sensed that God was opening a door for him—but he was hesitant. Speaking before a large group was one of his biggest fears. The Man took a deep breath and decided to do it.

Later that evening, the Man spent some time thinking about his testimony. There was so much he wanted to say to these men. But who was he to lecture them? He was still trying to figure things out, and he had made many mistakes. He decided to write down what he had learned:

God's compassion never ends.

Sexual sin is a choice.

Intimacy without honesty is impossible.

Sexual sin is a misguided search for intimacy.

Love doesn't demand its own way.

Growth is often painful

13

"Then the Lord put out his hand and touched my mouth;
And the Lord said to me, 'Now I have put my words
in your mouth."
—Jeremiah 1:9

T he Man checked in at the hotel and went to his room. He took out the testimony he was going to deliver at the Workshop and read it out loud. He had to stop several times because he was overcome with emotion. It was exactly the message he wanted to deliver. He had asked God to direct his hand, and God had helped him bare his soul. As uncomfortable as he was about speaking before a large group, he was at peace knowing that this is what God had brought him here to do. That evening, he was surprisingly calm as he walked up to the lectern to tell his story to an audience of 100 men:

> *I have been sexually sober for 15 months and 23 days. (Applause) I'm very proud of that. As odd as it might sound, quitting was the easy part. Living with the consequences of my sin has been much harder. When I attended this Workshop more than a year ago, I knew that pornography had been slowly destroying me and that my marriage was crumbling. I was confused and I was desperate. In my desperation, I turned to God. I saw myself as a victim of a compulsion I couldn't control. The reality was that I*

had chosen to let pornography take over my life, to separate me from God and from my wife, and from the man I really was.

When I returned home, I opened up to my wife completely. I was so filled with remorse over what I had done to her, to our marriage, and to myself that my tears flowed freely. I told her what I was going to do to make things right between us and, more important, that I had to make things right with God for my own sake. As much as I had hurt her, she felt good that finally I was being honest with her and allowing myself to be vulnerable. One night she even invited me to dance in our living room. It was as if all the barriers between us had vanished and all the hurt had been washed away. It was a lovely moment, and I wish it could have lasted. For now, it's a fond memory that I hope we can relive someday.

It's funny, but in the beginning, when I thought I had little hope of saving my marriage, I found it easy to be open and honest, and it felt wonderful. But when I began to believe my wife would stay and try to work things through, I became more careful about sharing my feelings. Old fears that she might not love me if she really knew me resurfaced. How could I reveal that I felt scared or confused when she needed me to be strong? The harder I tried to appear perfect, the more she doubted I was being honest and the more she feared I was hiding something, that maybe I was weakening. I'm learning that my only hope is to risk opening *my heart.*

There have been many times over the past year when I have wondered whether our marriage would survive. Early on I decided that I couldn't control whether my wife would choose to stay with me, but I could control my behavior with God's help. I knew that God had to forgive me if I repented and turned away from my sin. He had to take me back. It said so in the Bible. When my wife and I had terrible arguments, I sometimes feared that God might take her away so I would seek him as desperately as I had done when my sin was first uncovered.

I've been seeing a therapist for about a year now, and he's helped me to confront a lot of issues of self-worth that have haunted me since childhood, when my grandmother would verbally abuse me. I had not realized how damaging her words had been and how they were still affecting my life. He also has helped me explore how I developed some unhealthy attitudes about sex and love. My wife has attended some sessions with me to try to heal the deep wounds my behavior has caused and to try to build a healthy relationship, but that has not been easy to do.

Even though we've made progress, her doubts remain. I often react to her questioning with anger, which only makes things worse. I know she wants to trust me, but she's afraid of being hurt again. Some days I'm angry we have to go through this, and some days I can't even feel the joy that I should feel about the good things in my life.

Most days I feel like I'm failing, even though I have abandoned pornography. It is hell to live this way.

My life will never be the same again, and that is a good thing, because it had been built on a lie. I had fancied myself a good husband and father, a good Christian, a church leader. To all appearances, that is who I was. But I was also a man who regularly turned to pornography to escape from who he thought he was—a person unworthy of love. Over the past year, my wife has seen me at my worst and somehow she still loves me.

This past summer, I told my daughter, 20, and my sons, 18 and 33, that I've been going to counseling because I've had a problem with pornography that has hurt their mother deeply and almost destroyed our marriage. It was one of the most difficult things I've ever had to do. I agonized for weeks about what to say to them. What would they think of me? I finally worked up the courage to tell them— and guess what? They still love me. My deepest fear—and part of the reason I turned to pornography—has been that if anyone really knew me, they wouldn't love me. I was wrong about that.

We still have a lot to work through, but I am a stronger person for having confronted this problem. My faith has been severely tested, but God has never left my side. I am blessed to have a wife of incredible strength and faith who loves me as I am. Last week, she gave me a photo to show my therapist. My son at age five is on my lap, and we have

big smiles on our faces. She wanted to show
him that I used to be a happy guy. With
God's help, I will be a happy guy again.

When the Man was finished, everyone in the room stood and applauded. When he returned to his seat, a young man sitting next to him—who he had not met before—put his hand on the Man's shoulder and said, "Thank you." He was crying. The Man had never felt so right about anything he had ever done in his life. After the session, another man came up to him and shook his hand.

"That was powerful," he said. "I heard several guys today wondering out loud if what they've heard over the past few days could actually work." The Man's words had reassured them.

As soon as he got back to his room, the Man rejoiced in the miracle that God had performed. God had helped him put aside his fears to deliver a message of hope and repentance. God had used his pain and suffering for good. The Man offered a grateful prayer, "Thank you for using me, Lord, to carry your word and healing power." Tears filled his eyes as he finally accepted an important truth:

I am precious in God's sight.

14

*"When my soul was embittered, when I was pricked in heart,
I was stupid and ignorant; I was like a brute
beast toward you."*
—Psalm 73:21-22

It was late afternoon, and the hospital room was quiet. The Man sat at his father's bedside, watching him die. The doctors had given his father days, maybe a week. The Man felt nothing. He was emotionless in a moment that cried out for emotion. The anger he had directed toward his father for so long had turned to indifference. He recalled a happy childhood moment at the park with his dad, but it was a lifeless snapshot in time.

The Man called the Pastor and asked him to come by to give his father a chance to make his peace with God. As he waited for the Pastor to arrive, the Man studied a photo of his father in uniform at age 20 and wondered: *What were his hopes and dreams?*

Over the years, the Man had tried to bury his feelings about his father. His father had not defended him when he was a child; he had rarely stood up to the Man's mother. He could not forgive his father for that. In spite of his feelings, the Man had played the role of the dutiful son. He had looked after his father ever since a stroke made it a necessity. The Man wondered if God might be orchestrating this final scene to teach him something.

The following morning, the Man visited the Pastor to talk about the emotions—and the lack of emotion—he felt toward his father. The Pastor told him to accept his feelings for what they were: real. Not perfect, not loving, not even desirable, but real. The Man pictured his father lying helpless in a hospital bed and realized that he had judged him harshly. He knew how tough it was to be a good father, and it was God's place, not his, to render the ultimate judgment. The indifference he had felt toward his father was turning to compassion.

The Man told the Pastor about a horrible vision he had the day before. The Man was dying, and the Sons and the Daughter were standing over him, feeling no love in their hearts. The Pastor said it was natural that the Man would project himself into the future this way.

"The most important thing we can do," he said, "is to be sure we are showing our love to our children." If the Man's parents did not display affection openly, the Pastor said, it was not something that would come naturally to him. The abuse the Man suffered as a child also made it hard for him to show vulnerability. They prayed together for a while, and the Man left feeling better.

A week later, the family watched a video in which a Christian speaker told a large gathering of women that as a young man he had gotten a girl pregnant and pressured her to have an abortion. Years later, when he and his wife learned they were unable to have a baby, he believed that God was denying him a child as punishment for his sin. He then delivered an emotional story of how they were able to adopt a baby girl, which proved to him that his God was a God of second chances. It was a moving presentation.

The next afternoon, the Man and the Son went kayaking. They paddled about a hundred yards from the shore then drifted quietly for a bit, enjoying the warmth of the sun on their faces.

"What did you think of the video last night?" The Man asked, breaking the silence. He hadn't planned to bring it up. He was just making conversation.

"It was good," the Son responded with his usual economy of words.

"I thought it was a powerful message," said the Man. "You know, how God can forgive anything, even something as awful as aborting a child."

"That would be a hard decision to have to make," the Son said. "What do you think you'd do if that happened to you?" He asked the question so casually. He couldn't have known.

Without thinking, the Man blurted out, "That did happen to me." His candidness surprised him. Normally, he would have carefully considered whether to reveal such a personal secret.

"Whaaaat?" the Son responded, with a nervous laugh.

The Man told him the whole story. When they were heading back to shore, the Man said, "I'd like you to feel that you can talk to me about anything."

"That would be nice," the Son said.

The Man had always demonstrated his love for his wife and children the way many men do—by providing for them, fixing things around the house, and performing other manly duties. These were legitimate expressions of love, but the Man now saw that they were not enough. He needed to display his love and affection outwardly. He started by sending the Daughter an e-mail to say he loved her and was thinking about her. What he would have given for such a show of his parents' love.

As the weeks passed, he slowly began to reach out to others. One Sunday he approached a church member and complimented him on his speaking voice. The Man had often thought about such kind gestures but had not acted on them. It seemed that everywhere he looked, there were opportunities to express love. He found that he liked himself better when he opened his heart. The Man had learned another lesson:

The more love you give, the more there is to give.

15

"Blessed is anyone who endures temptation."
—James 1:12

On a chilly spring morning, the Man sat on the porch and read his journal. He had buried his father two weeks ago, and he was going over what he had written during the last days of his father's life.

Tomorrow, he would be seeing the Therapist for the last time before the family moved back home. The Man thought about how he had grown over the past year and a half. He had resolved his anger toward his father. He had grieved his mother's death. He had forgiven his grandmother for years of verbal abuse. He had told his children he had a problem with pornography. He had given his testimony to a group of 100 men. He was praying and reading the Bible every day. He was a different person now, someone he did not despise anymore for being weak.

If he had one regret, it was that he had not been honest with the Woman about his struggles with temptation. It was true that ever since she had caught him on that fateful night, he had had no desire to look at pornography on the Internet. It was as if he had touched a hot stove and gotten severely burned and was terrified of ever going near a stove again.

But sexual temptation was everywhere—on TV, on bill-boards, on the street, in store windows, in the mailbox. He was proud that the Son and the Daughter had seen him change the channel or walk out of the room whenever anything remotely provocative came on. Still, the Man felt he was in a Catch-22: if he admitted that he still wrestled with temptation, the Woman would fear that their situation was hopeless; if he insisted that he was never tempted, she would doubt him. Her doubts often led to accusations, which brought out his anger. Patience was not the Man's strong suit.

"What am I supposed to do when the Woman accuses me of something I didn't do?" the Man asked the Therapist. "I get frustrated because I can't prove my innocence. And when I get angry about it, the Woman thinks I have something to hide."

The Therapist thought for a moment.

"Instead of trying to reassure her in the heat of an argument," he said, "you should sit her down in a calm moment and remind her that you have not used pornography for more than a year. Tell her how good you feel about that and renew your commitment to her and to God."

The Man left the Therapist's office and immediately turned his thoughts to the upcoming move. In three weeks, he and the Woman would be heading toward what they hoped would be a new life. When he got in his car, he jotted down three things:

Temptation is inevitable.

Even Jesus was tempted.

Temptation is not sin.

16

"For if they fall, one will lift up the other;
But woe to one who is alone and falls
And does not have another to help."
—Ecclesiastes 4:9-10

Soon after the dust from the move had settled, the Man and the Woman began to argue about the same things. Their arguing upset the Son and the Daughter, who were now living at home and going to school nearby. They were sad that the Man and the Woman were not happy; they had hoped things would be different here.

The Man had wanted to believe that he and the Woman were finished with the hurt and mistrust, but they were not. They were back home now, and they had been excited about a new beginning. He had wanted to turn the page and move on.

He had kept his promises to God and to the Woman for almost two years, and he did not want to accept that he was still in recovery. Any reminder of it made him angry. His sullen and sour behavior frightened the Woman. Her biggest fear had been that he would return to his old habits.

At times, the Man felt overwhelmed, and he was often discouraged and fearful. But he continued to believe that if he remained true to God, then God would remain true to him. He had again made it hard for the Woman to love him, and he couldn't blame her for the way she felt.

"You don't make me feel special," she had said last night in the middle of another argument.

The Man had tried to defend himself, but he knew she was right. He had not been willing to go the extra mile and do the little romantic things that showed he cared. Despite the difficulties they were facing, he took it for granted that she would be strong enough and have enough faith to endure. He knew he should be on his knees, thanking God for her and making her life as happy as he could, instead of expecting her to comfort him.

After many weeks, the Woman had had enough. She insisted that the Man find someone to talk to on a regular basis, as he had done with the Pastor and the Therapist before the move. He knew she was right. A local Christian counselor arranged for him to meet a new Accountability Partner for lunch, and the two men quickly bonded.

Because the Man was farther along in recovery, he looked forward to helping his Accountability Partner avoid some of the mistakes he had made. It felt good to talk to someone who didn't judge him. He had missed his conversations with the Pastor and with the Therapist, but he had been reluctant to tell his story to anyone new. The Man and the Accountability Partner talked about how they dealt with particular temptations and went over a list of questions that addressed their commitment to sexual sobriety. The Man was glad to have someone to pray with and to share his struggles.

The Woman immersed herself in her work and her children. With her marriage faltering, she wanted to feel successful at something. They were in a new church and had not yet gotten involved in serving others, as they had done at their previous church. The Man and the Woman decided to begin praying together every morning and separately for each other, and they read the Bible each night before they went to sleep.

The Woman also took comfort in being around so much that was familiar. The other day, they had driven past the house where she had had such a happy childhood. They had also driven through the Man's old neighborhood, and when they passed the house where he spent the first ten years of his life, the Woman had thought about the stories he had told her about his grandmother. She was finally seeing the place where the Man had experienced some of the worst times of his life. She was amazed at his upbeat demeanor as he talked about his childhood. It was as if he had blocked out all the painful memories.

In a moment of compassion, the Woman considered forgiving the Man. She knew that Jesus had forgiven those who had betrayed him. She had read that forgiveness meant showing love and kindness to the one who had hurt you, and she felt she had done this. She had also read that forgiveness meant you no longer sought revenge. She knew that was an area that needed work. There still were times she wanted the Man to suffer. She wanted him to hurt like she was hurting. She decided she was not ready to forgive.

The Man opened an old hymnal and began to read the words of some of his favorite hymns. He recalled a sermon about turning your thoughts toward the things of God to help you in times of temptation. He had been tempted to be angry today, but he had filled his mind with words of comfort and the anger had disappeared.

A few days later, the Man realized he had been insensitive to the Woman and rebellious toward God. She had asked him for months to renew his commitment to her as he did each week with his Accountability Partner. She needed reassurance, and he had withheld it. He now understood why: He had resented her for asking. He knew he had been doing all the right things. Wasn't that enough? Why should he have to do more? The answer was simply that the Woman deserved it, but his pride had gotten in the way. He could see that he was not the selfless husband he thought he was. He remembered an old friend's favorite passage from Scripture:

"I am confident of this, that the one who began a good work among you will bring it to completion by the day of Jesus Christ."
(Philippians 1:6)

The Man knew that God was not finished with him yet. He recalled a session with the Therapist early in recovery when he had complained that the Woman got mad because he had taken so long at the grocery.

"Why does she need to know my every move?" the Man had asked. "I wasn't doing anything wrong. It really ticks me off to have to defend myself all the time."

"This is all about trust," the Therapist had replied. "The way to build trust is by being accountable—being where you are supposed to be, doing what you are supposed to be doing. Over time, the Woman will grow to feel more secure about trusting you."

The Man shook his head. More than two years had passed, and the Woman still had doubts. Instead of being disheartened, he thanked God for giving the Woman the strength to stay with him. He thanked God for his children, for a roof over his head, for food to eat, for his family's health, for their new church. He thanked God for sending him an Accountability Partner to help him reconnect with his wound.

The Man picked up his journal and wrote down four things:

Accountability builds trust.

Rebuilding trust takes time.

Recovery never ends.

You can't make it alone.

17

*"Bear with one another and, if anyone has
a complaint against another,
Forgive each other; just as the Lord has forgiven you,
you also must forgive."*
—Colossians 3:13

The topic of this morning's sermon was forgiveness.
"If we don't forgive those who have sinned against us,"
the Pastor said, "we will remain a prisoner of the sin."

Although the Woman felt she had forgiven the Man
some time ago by showing him love, she knew she had at
times displayed tremendous anger, even hatred. She had
wondered how those awful feelings could resurface so
easily.

"Prisoner...Prisoner...Prisoner." The Pastor kept repeating the word. The Woman feared that at any moment he
would insert her name in his sermon. She knew she had to
release her burden and deliver the words she believed the
Man needed to hear.

Later that day, she invited the Man out into the back
yard and handed him a yellow sheet of paper, folded to form
a homemade greeting card. On the front, she had drawn a
heart with an arrow through it. Inside the heart, she had
written their initials.

The Man opened the card and read her words:

My Sweet,
    I don't want any more pain, anger,
resentment, or mistrust in our life. I know

109

I've said that I didn't need to say the words "I forgive you" because of the love I've shown you. But I was wrong. I think that what the Pastor preached about forgiveness this morning is true. As of this day, I forgive you and want to begin anew. What do you say? I love you.

The Man smiled and looked up at her. He knew how hard this was for her to do. For a long time, he had thought that he needed to receive those words, but he had come to understand that she had needed to write them far more. The Man had prayed often—and again during the morning's sermon—that God would give the Woman peace. He thanked God for answering his prayer. Her inability to forgive had kept her trapped in a cycle of anger and resentment. Now she was free.

Although it was the Daughter's twenty-second birthday, the Man knew he would always remember this as the day the Woman forgave him. Two years, five months, and eleven days had passed since he had delivered a devastating blow to their marriage. They had both learned something about forgiveness:

Without forgiveness, you cannot release the past.

18

"So if anyone is in Christ, there is a new creation;
Everything old has passed away; see, everything has
become new."
—2 Corinthians 5:17

One night, the Man and the Woman went to dinner. She looked beautiful, and he could not take his eyes off of her. But he wasn't obsessed with the thought of making love to her as he had often been in the past. He was able to enjoy the music, dance some, and exchange tender glances.

As they headed home, the Man began to get frustrated, thinking that sex might not be in the cards. It was very late, and by the time they got into bed all the Woman wanted to do was snuggle and drift off to sleep. The Man lay in bed next to her, stewing silently.

"What's wrong?" the Woman asked, barely awake.

"I want to make love to you," he said, softly.

"I'd like that," she said, "but I'm so tired."

"It's okay," the Man said, and he meant it. He was glad he had told her how he felt, and he was satisfied with her caring response.

The next morning he got up early and went downstairs to read. He thought about how, in the past, he would have been grouchy all day because he hadn't gotten what he had wanted the night before. Instead, he thought about how radiant the Woman had been last night and how affectionately she had looked at him. Two and a half years ago, he would have given anything to see such an expression of love on her face, a look he thought he'd never see again. He choked up thinking back to those hopeless days. He offered a silent prayer of gratitude, "Thank you, Lord, for the gift of the Woman."

Another year passed, and more healing had taken place. The Man was closer to God now than he had been three and a half years ago, when he had fancied himself a church leader, even as he was wrapped in the cords of a wretched sin.

He had been a shadow Christian.

But since then the Man had searched his soul and had found that what was lacking had been an intimate connection with the God who created him. The Man sometimes teased the Woman by saying, "You are the second most important thing in my life," to which she would always respond, "I'm okay with that."

The Woman's faith also had blossomed. She had watched God transform their marriage and bless them throughout their ordeal. She had also regained respect for the Man because she had seen him remain true to his commitment to her and to God. They both were active in their church, and this had brought new friends into their lives.

And they laughed a lot more.

The Man and the Woman talked more openly about what it meant to have the kind of healthy physical relationship with each other that God intended. The Man had desired intimacy with his wife all along, but his dishonesty had taken him in the opposite direction. He no longer had any doubt that the Woman loved him deeply. She had shown him love even in their darkest moments.

The Man regularly set aside time for his children because he wanted them to know he loved them. The children had seen the Man and the Woman turn to God in a time of crisis, and they had seen God walk with them through the storm.

One afternoon the Man saw a bumper sticker that read, "Real Men Pray." He smiled as he pondered the message. Real men pray because real men know they need God. He came up with a few other things that real men do:

Real men tell the truth.

Real men admit their mistakes.

Real men are not ruled by their desires.

Real men respect their wives' boundaries.

Real men are spiritual leaders at home.

Real men help their wives blossom.

Real men give more than they take.

Real men aren't afraid to cry.

Real men are joyful.

Real men need God.

19

B ecause the Man was human, he still sometimes questioned what God was doing and why. Or when he wanted something, why God didn't do it more quickly. The Man often had doubts and fears, but when he did, he knew where to turn. He remembered that whenever he had relied on his own understanding, he had stumbled. The Man could now feel God's presence more intensely in his life.

It was the Sunday after Easter, and the service was nearly over. The Man, the Woman, the Son, and the Daughter rose with the congregation to sing "He Lives." The Man welled up with emotion as he began the second verse: *"In all the world around me, I see his loving care; and tho' my heart grows weary I never will despair...."* He turned to look at the Woman and she met his gaze. She had tears in her eyes. He smiled at her and took her hand. At that moment they both were certain of one thing:

They had to share what God had done for them.

About the Authors

Linda and Al share their inspiring story at conferences, churches, and colleges. Al served as Executive Director of the Atlanta office of the National Coalition for the Protection of Children and Families before he and Linda founded Shadow Christian Ministries. They also mentor individuals and couples and consult with churches on sexual issues. Linda and Al are Certified Pastoral Sexual Addiction Specialists, C.P.S.A.S. In 2011, they developed a ground-breaking model for couples groups that offer a unique mix of counseling and mentoring. They have been married for 32 years, have three grown children and one grandchild, and live in Marietta, Georgia.

TESTIMONIALS

"The mentoring Al and Linda provide is the missing piece we had been looking for." **RICHARD BLANKENSHIP** Cornerstone Professional Counseling Center, Atlanta

"People are still talking about how powerful your Sunday testimony was." **AARON GABLE**, Pastor, LifeBridge Church

"Al and Linda gave me hope and showed me I was not alone. This group gave me the push to keep going." **B.P.**

"You and Linda have forever impacted my life and my marriage. I treasure you both." **J.B.**

"Your words broke my stone-cold heart. My marriage is better than it's ever been. You changed my life." **D.G.**

"My love for my husband has deepened over the past six months. I love him in ways I never knew I could." **A.G.**

"Thank you for pouring your lives into ours. You've blessed us more than you can imagine." **C.D.**

TO CONTACT AL OR LINDA VISIT: THESHADOWCHRISTIAN.COM

STUDY GUIDE

Whether or not sexual sin has had a direct impact on your life, there is no denying the damage it is doing to marriages and families, cutting at the very heart of the church. Although this book focuses on one couple's experience, the issues it addresses are central to every believer's walk of faith, including transparency, repentance, forgiveness, and grace. Men and women from all walks of life have been deeply moved by this timeless tale of redemption.

As with any good story, it is best to read straight through from beginning to end. *The Shadow Christian* is no exception. If you have not done so already, we recommend that you read the entire story before moving to this guide.

Then, before going ahead with the first chapter of the study guide, reread Chapter 1 to prepare yourself for the questions and exercises. Repeat this process with each chapter as you move through the guide. After you have answered the questions and completed the exercises in a chapter, we encourage you to share your responses with a trusted friend, your spouse, or in a support group.

The Shadow Christian is also a great choice for small group study. We suggest answering the questions and completing the exercises between sessions and then using the responses to stimulate discussion on the issues each chapter addresses.

www.TheShadowChristian.com

Chapter 1

Nothing is covered up that will not be uncovered, and nothing secret that will not become known. (Luke 12:2)

As you were reading this chapter, what were you thinking and feeling about the Man?

What were you thinking and feeling about the Woman?

What stood out in your mind?

Excerpt: *It had been a day like any other for the Man, but his picture-perfect marriage was about to collapse.*

Just as you cannot judge a book by its cover, you cannot judge a person or a marriage by outward appearances. What kinds of masks do you put on to make yourself look good?

Think of a time when you told an outright lie, a half-truth, or withheld the truth and thought you would get away with it. Did the truth eventually come out? Describe the circumstances.

Think about some secret sins that you have committed in your life. If they have not already come to light, do you fear that one day they will?

What can you do right now to address those sins?

Excerpt: *"How could you do this?" she asked, her voice trembling. The Man tried to defend himself and said, "Maybe if we had sex more often, I wouldn't have needed to." He knew his words were unfair.*

When confronted with something you've done wrong, are you more likely to admit you were wrong and apologize, or deny your guilt, try to justify your actions, minimize the extent of what you've done, or blame someone else, all of which are common forms of denial?

In what areas of your life might you be in denial about your behavior?

Excerpt: *All she knew for sure right now was that she couldn't live with a man who couldn't live without pornography.*

In the midst of chaos, the Woman did not waver on what she believed was and was not acceptable. Why is it important to have clearly defined standards of behavior?

Do your standards line up with God's word, or do they more closely mirror the world's values?

List your three most deeply held values by completing this simple sentence:

I believe....

I believe....

I believe....

Now list the source of each of those values.

When have you compromised your values to hold on to a relationship?

In what areas of your life are you allowing the world to shape your values?

Excerpt: *The Man awoke at 4:30 a.m. and began to read the*

Bible. He was looking for some sign that God could forgive him. He stopped when he came to this passage: "Just so, I tell you, there will be more joy in heaven over one sinner who repents than over ninety-nine righteous persons who need no repentance." (Luke 15:7)

Do you believe that God will forgive you for whatever sins you have committed, if only you will confess them to Him? Why or why not?

Chapter 2

Wretched man that I am! Who will rescue me from this body of death? (Romans 7:24)

As you read through this chapter, what were you thinking and feeling about the Man?

What were you thinking and feeling about the Woman?

What stood out in your mind?

Excerpt: *Hadn't he been introduced to sex like most boys of his generation, through the photos in* Playboy *magazine? He had ogled women as far back as he could remember. Wasn't this his entitlement as a red-blooded American male?*

What was your earliest exposure to sex?

Do you remember it as a positive or negative experience?

Do you think viewing pornography is a private issue that doesn't hurt anyone? Why or why not?

Excerpt: *By Thanksgiving night, the charade was wearing*

thin, and the Woman accused the Man of having an *affair*. *"I've never been unfaithful to you,"* the Man *responded. "What you've done on the Internet is the same thing,"* the Woman shot back. *"Doesn't the Bible say that if a man lusts in his heart he is committing adultery?"*

Do you believe a person can commit "emotional" infidelity? Why or why not?

If you answered yes to the previous question, do you also believe that emotional infidelity can be just as hurtful as a physical affair? Why or why not?

What areas of your life do you need to release to God's control?

Repentance means not only turning away from sin but also turning toward God. List areas of your life that you still try to control.

Excerpt: *The Man felt a profound emptiness, as if the Woman's trust were a living organism that had been ripped from deep inside of him.*

In that moment, the Man doubted the Woman would

ever trust him again. Have you ever felt hopeless? Describe the circumstances and outcome.

How do you typically handle pain and disappointment?

Excerpt: *After last night, he was only sure of one thing: He needed a miracle.*

What do you believe about God?

Do you believe that God can work a miracle in someone's life? Why or why not?

Have you ever witnessed dramatic changes in someone that you previously thought would have been impossible? Describe what happened.

Do you believe that God could work a miracle in your life? Why or why not?

Chapter 3

Therefore confess your sins to one another, and pray for one another, so that you may be healed. (James 5:16)

As you read through this chapter, what were you thinking and feeling about the Man?

What were you thinking and feeling about the Woman?

What stood out in your mind?

Excerpt: *The first small group session was tomorrow, and the Man was not eager to share his secret with anyone. But he was here, and he would do whatever was necessary.*

Why is it essential for us to confess our sins? List some benefits.

Have you ever revealed a very personal secret about yourself? What were the circumstances?

How did the other person or persons react?

How did it feel to get it out in the open?

Do you have someone in your life with whom you can be completely honest, someone who will listen and not judge, someone who will be brutally honest and tell you when your thinking or actions are off-base?

If you answered no, how might you go about developing such a relationship?

Excerpt: *With the Man gone, the Woman felt a sense of freedom. It was the first time in a month that she could take a deep breath and try to absorb what was happening. She had wanted the Man out of the house and out of her life. She was finally going to have some peace. She wanted to forget about pornography and the damage it was doing to them and to millions of other families.*

Actions have consequences, and our sexual behavior is no exception. List some of the consequences the Man and the Woman had to face as a result of his actions.

Excerpt: *The Man had tried to tell himself he was a victim of his sexual desires, but today he could not deny that each time he had fantasized about women—whether they were walking down the street, in magazines, on television, or on the Internet—he had made a deliberate choice.*

Have you ever seen yourself as a victim rather than taking responsibility for the choices you made? Describe the circumstances.

Excerpt: *At that moment, the Man realized that out of love for him, God had exposed his sin and forced him to deal with it.*

How is it actually an expression of love when God reveals areas of our lives that are not only hurting us and others, but are standing in the way of a deeper relationship with Him?

Chapter 4

Those who love me I will deliver; I will protect those who know my name. When they call to me, I will answer them; I will be with them in trouble, I will rescue them and honor them. (Psalm 91:14-15)

As you read through this chapter, what were you thinking and feeling about the Man?

What were you thinking and feeling about the Woman?

What stood out in your mind?

Excerpt: *The Leader went on, "Your behavior has shaken your loved one's confidence and taken away her sense of safety." The Man closed his eyes and imagined the Woman, alone in their house, looking sad, lost, and scared. "She is having doubts about herself. She is feeling stupid for ever trusting you, and she's having to ask herself, 'Why would God give me a man in marriage who would break my heart?'"*

Whenever we hurt someone, we often focus on the impact it will have on ourselves. Why is it crucial to appreciate, as best you can, the depth of hurt you have caused someone and the consequences they will have to face as a result of your actions?

What is the difference between feeling guilt and feeling remorse?

Excerpt: *When the Woman spoke, the Man could hear anger in her voice. She had had a day and a half alone to think and search for answers. She told him she had been reading about sexual addiction, and some of what she had read seemed to say that men were helpless victims of sexual temptation, which made her furious. She had also read that men usually try to blame their wives. She guaranteed him that she was not going to let him make her feel guilty or doubt herself.*

When sexual sin was revealed in your life, describe how you reacted.

Make a list of words that describe how you felt at the time.

FOR THE ONE WHO SINNED:

> Did you try to blame someone else or try to make them feel guilty?

FOR THE ONE WHO WAS BETRAYED:

Did you initially experience any feelings of guilt?

Did you begin to doubt that you were attractive enough, which is an understandable reaction under these circumstances?

If you answered yes to either or both questions, have you since come to understand that those feelings were unjustified?

Excerpt: *The Man had wanted closeness, but he had been unwilling to let the Woman know him. He had wanted her to see him not as he was, but as he thought he ought to be—so he lied, even about small things.*

God created us for an intimate relationship with Him and with others. Why is it hard sometimes to reveal our true selves to those we care about?

Why is it impossible to have true intimacy without honesty?

Excerpt: *The Woman was not ready for the man to come home tomorrow. She wondered how she could have been so clueless about her husband's Jekyll and Hyde behavior. How could she have been so blind?*

With sexual sin, deception is always part of the equation.

FOR THE ONE WHO SINNED:

> Describe the feeling of relief you experienced when your sin was exposed.

FOR THE ONE WHO WAS BETRAYED:

> Looking back, were there any red flags in your relationship that you chose to ignore? If so, list them.

Excerpt: *Even though the Man had failed his wife and had sinned again and again, God had never stopped loving him. The Man felt tears form in his eyes.*

There are more than a hundred verses in the Bible about God's unfailing love. For example, Psalm 66:20 says, "Praise God, who did not ignore my prayer or withdraw his unfailing love from me." Can you accept in your heart that God loves you in spite of the mistakes you have made?

If you are having trouble with this, is there someone you could talk with who might be able to help you accept God's love? (If not, you can get help at www.theshadowchristian. com.)

Chapter 5

We are afflicted in every way, but not crushed; perplexed, but not driven to despair; persecuted, but not forsaken; struck down, but not destroyed. (2 Corinthians 4:8-9)

As you read through this chapter, what were you thinking and feeling about the Man?

What were you thinking and feeling about the Woman?

What stood out in your mind?

Excerpt: *"I want to be completely honest with you for the first time in our marriage," he said. Tears ran down his cheeks, but he made no attempt to hide them. He didn't try to compose himself, as he normally would have done. The Woman had never seen him like this.*

Has there been a time in your life when you chose or were forced to bare your soul? Describe what happened.

Have you ever thought that if someone knew the real you, they wouldn't love you?

Excerpt: *The Man read her a list of changes he was going to make. The list included joining a support group, seeing a*

Christian therapist, installing an Internet filter, finding an accountability partner, reading the Bible at least five minutes a day, and more. The man made a commitment to the Woman and to God to carry out these changes.

Trust is the first casualty of sexual sin, and trust is the hardest to restore. List some commitments you are willing to make to become more trustworthy.

If you are the one whose trust was violated, list some commitments you would like to see the other person make to you.

Excerpt: *But the Woman could not see into his heart. She could not know the loneliness he had felt because of his sin, the moments of deep despair, or the closeness he had experienced with God while he was away.*

Have you ever experienced loneliness as a result of having sinned? If yes, describe how you felt.

What do you typically do when you feel alone?

What periods of adversity have you managed to work through in your life?

What part, if any, did God play during those periods?

What kinds of stresses are you facing right now?

Excerpt: *The Man sought God each day by studying the lives of great men of Scripture, including King David, and found that even the most blessed of men had disappointed God. David had done terrible things and yet God had forgiven him and continued to use him to accomplish great things. David had also paid a price for disobeying God, and so had he.*

King David committed adultery and later arranged to have the woman's husband killed to cover his tracks before he eventually repented for his sins. Why is it helpful to learn about the strengths—and weaknesses—of those whom God chose to carry out His purposes?

Why do you think God selected ordinary people, such as fishermen and shepherds, rather than the elite of society?

How can knowing that King David committed adultery and murder yet was forgiven be a source of hope for every sinner?

Excerpt: *"Why haven't you found a therapist yet?" the Woman asked.*
"You know I've been looking," the Man said.

"If it was important to you," she said, "you would have found one." She was furious that he had not taken care of this, and she was beginning to doubt that the changes he had made were genuine.

How has pride kept you from seeking help when you've needed it?

Why is it essential to express humility after you have wronged someone?

Do you think that the Woman's anger was justified? Why?

Chapter 6

Trust in the Lord with all your heart and lean not on your own understanding. In all your ways acknowledge Him, and He will direct your paths. (Proverbs 3:5-6)

As you read through this chapter, what were you thinking and feeling about the Man?

What were you thinking and feeling about the Woman?

What stood out in your mind?

Excerpt: *The Therapist was about the same age as the Man and dealt with sexual issues from a Christian perspective. After a few minutes, the Man sensed that he had found someone who could help him. The Man recounted the events that had led him here, described the Workshop, and described where he and the Woman were in their relationship and in their lives.*

Looking back on your life, list some of the key events that shaped your views about love and sex.

Complete this sentence: "I sometimes feel uncomfortable talking about sex because...

Complete this sentence: "Sometimes I feel that sex is unfulfilling because...

Would you benefit from talking with someone who has experience with sexual issues/addiction? If so, contact us today at www.TheShadowChristian.com.)

Excerpt: *The Therapist suggested that the man list his good qualities and accomplishments for next time. Later that night, the Man worked on his assignment, but he could not come up with anything good to say about himself. The weight of his sin was crushing him. In his mind, whatever good he had done was now buried beneath a mountain of failure.*

List some of your good qualities and accomplishments.

Excerpt: *The Therapist listened intently as the Man talked about his longstanding desire to be in control of things, even as he recounted the ways his life had been tragically out of control for a long time.*

Consider the ways you seek to control other people and situations and write your thoughts.

Are there people in your life who you feel are controlling you?

If you answered yes, list them and describe how they exert control over you.

Do you resent any or all of these people?

What actions could you take to make these relationships more balanced?

Excerpt: *"The Woman said the other night that she has often felt used, and that I've seen her simply as a body to satisfy my needs," the Man said.*
"Can you blame her?" the Therapist asked. The Man was ashamed. It hurt him to know he had made the Woman feel that way.

At this point in the story, the Therapist suggested that the Man and the Woman abstain from sex of any kind for two weeks to give them a chance to relax with each other and learn to express affection for each other in non-sexual ways. A defined period of abstinence such as this has a sound biblical basis: *Do not deprive one another except with consent for a time, that you may give yourselves to fasting and prayer; and come together again so that Satan does not tempt you because of your lack of self-control.* (1 Corinthians 7:5)

List ways a person could communicate love to someone

else without being sexual.

Have you conditioned yourself to see sex as the primary way to feel loved? If so, how has that limited your ability to receive love in other ways?

Have you ever felt used? Describe the emotions that elicits.

Excerpt: *The Woman welcomed the chance to remove sex from the equation. Whenever she had heard someone on Christian radio talk about how God wanted married couples to enjoy a healthy sex life and that wives were supposed to surrender themselves, she had wanted to scream. Under the circumstances, how could she feel comfortable being the "dutiful wife"? What about her self-respect? How could she be expected to be intimate with her husband when the thought of sex elicited such anger and hurt?*

Do you believe the Woman's feelings were justified? Why?

Chapter 7

For if you live according to the flesh, you will die; but if by the Spirit you put to death the deeds of the body, you will live. (Romans 8:13)

As you read through this chapter, what were you thinking and feeling about the Man?

What were you thinking and feeling about the Woman?

What stood out in your mind?

Excerpt: *Two weeks had passed, and the Man hoped that abstaining from sex had convinced the Woman that he could be attentive without having an ulterior motive. He had been counting the days, which he realized was an indication that he was still preoccupied with sex.*

How much does sex dominate your thinking on a daily basis?

List some of the ways you fuel your lust on an average day. Think about what you see, where you go, what you watch, what you listen to, what you read.

How might your focus on sex diminish if you reduced or

eliminated some of these activities, including installing Internet filtering and accountability software?

How might your focus on sex diminish if you were more fulfilled in other aspects of your life?

Excerpt: *The Woman was coming with the Man to see the Therapist for the first time. He had invited her before, but she had not been ready. She had joked that it was his head that needed to be examined, not hers.*

Why was it a good idea for the Woman to attend some therapy sessions with the Man?

Excerpt: *The Woman was apprehensive. She didn't know what to expect. Ever since she had learned about the Man's betrayal, she had not been able to cry, and this was unusual.*

List changes you have seen in your behavior as a result of sexual sin being revealed in your life.

Excerpt: *Over the weeks that followed, the Man began to treat the Woman differently. He would softly touch her face and tell her how beautiful she was. In the morning, he would cuddle with her and gently stroke her hair. He saw that his obsession with sex had robbed them of this kind of closeness.*

How have your views about sex and love robbed you of the true intimacy you desire?

Chapter 8

For I will restore health to you, and your wounds I will heal, says the Lord. (Jeremiah 30:17)

As you read through this chapter, what were you thinking and feeling about the Man?

What were you thinking and feeling about the Woman?

What stood out in your mind?

Excerpt: *"I cry all the time," the Man told the Therapist. "I cry when I think of all the hurt the Woman is feeling. I cry for no reason sometimes. I can't seem to focus on work."*
"You're grieving the loss of your old way of life," the Therapist replied. Sexual acting out was something you could count on to dull the pain and relieve stress. And now it's gone."

Now that the Man had stopped using sex to cope with emotional pain and stress, he had to find alternatives. List some healthy ways to deal with emotional pain and stress.

Excerpt: *During this period of grieving, the Therapist said, other unresolved issues might surface.*

Think about the important relationships in your life. Are there any unresolved issues between you and any of these individuals?

List each person and the issue that is unresolved.

What actions can you take to begin to address these unresolved issues? (If the person is deceased, write a letter telling them what is on your heart.)

Excerpt: *The Man was aware that he had wrapped many protective layers around himself, and he knew it would take time to peel them away. He felt as if the Woman wanted to take a hot poker and burn through them all at once.*

Identify any protective layers you have wrapped around yourself to keep others from knowing your true feelings.

How can you begin to remove those layers of protection and express your true feelings?

What is your biggest fear in revealing your true self to those who are close to you?

Excerpt: *The Man felt as if he were going to explode. Their world was collapsing and he could do nothing to prevent it.*

In times of crisis, it often feels as if the situation will only get worse. What can you do to let God into your crisis and direct your steps?

How can cultivating a spirit of patience help you in times of crisis?

Excerpt: *The Man knew he had broken the Woman's heart, yet she was sitting here beside him in the Therapist's office. She had refused to accept his sinful behavior and had forced him to confront it, which was another expression of love. The Man thanked God for the Woman. He could see that she was a model for other women in this situation.*

Why is unconditional love, as demonstrated here by the Woman, the highest form of love?

How often do you put conditions on your love? For example, your child might say, "Mom and Dad will only love me if I get straight A's."

Are there people in your life who put conditions on their love for you? If so, write their names and what conditions they impose.

I Corinthians 13:7 says, *Love bears all things, believes all things, hopes all things, endures all things.* What positives can you identify as a result of enduring previous trials in your life?

Chapter 9

I praise you, for I am fearfully and wonderfully made. Wonderful are your works; that I know very well. (Psalm 139: 14)

As you read through this chapter, what were you thinking and feeling about the Man?

What were you thinking and feeling about the Woman?

What stood out in your mind?

Excerpt: *"The child who thinks he's no good does not want to let go of the image he has held on to for so long,"* the Therapist said. *"Whenever you begin to change that image, he becomes uncomfortable and tries to sabotage what you're doing."*

As you begin to change how you think and act to align yourself with the will of God, you must expect the Enemy to push back, by reminding you of past failures and trying to convince you that you cannot change. What negative thoughts about yourself are you still holding on to?

Read and memorize these verses to remind yourself how

God sees you:

"I chose you when I planned creation." (Ephesians 1:11-12)
"You are fearfully and wonderfully made." (Psalm 139:14)
"My plan for your future has always been filled with hope." (Jeremiah 29:11)
"As a shepherd carries a lamb, I have carried you close to my heart." (Isaiah 40:11)
"I am your Father, and I love you even as I love my son, Jesus." (John 17:23)

To help yourself focus on how God has blessed you, list 100 things for which you are thankful.

Select items from your list of blessings and turn them into prayers of thanksgiving. Example: "Lord, I am thankful for...

Excerpt: (Midway through this chapter, the Man acknowledged to the Woman that he had buried the memory of how his grandmother verbally abused him as a child.) *"I guess I've avoided going deeper because I didn't want to feel the pain again." The Therapist had said that the Man needed to feel the hurt so he could accept that what had happened was real. Once he accepted that it was real, he could forgive his grandmother.*

What hurts have you buried to avoid feeling the pain all over again?

How have these hurts affected the way you think about yourself and how you behave toward others, especially those you care most about?

Excerpt: *The Man and the Woman had been able to disguise their feelings when their children had visited on breaks and weekends. Now they could not conceal the fact that their marriage was in crisis.*

When sexual sin occurs in your life, it's easy to delude yourself into thinking that how you behave is not having an impact on those closest to you, including your children. What are you communicating to those closest to you by the way you are dealing with your current difficulties?

Have you noticed any changes in their behavior? If so, list them.

What changes in your own behavior might you need to make?

Chapter 10

We also boast in our sufferings, knowing that suffering produces endurance, and endurance produces character, and character produces hope. (Romans 5:3-4)

As you read through this chapter, what were you thinking and feeling about the Man?

What were you thinking and feeling about the Woman?

What stood out in your mind?

Excerpt: *As he sat alone in the dark, the Man recalled the time the Woman described their arguing as a "setback" at one of their sessions. "How is that a setback?" the Therapist had asked, raising his eyebrows. He reminded them that they had communicated their needs and fears to each other and insisted, "That is a sign of growth."*

It is often true that the positive changes that have occurred in your life can get overshadowed by unpleasant memories from the past. During these times, you may feel as if you are back at square one. But that is not the reality. List some of the positive changes you have seen in your life and review them daily.

Now list some new potential areas of growth.

Why do you think growth is often painful?

Excerpt: *The Man walked outside and stood in the sun for a while. Sweat trickled down his arms, and in the calm he thought of one of his favorite verses of Scripture: "Be still and know that I am God." (Psalm 46:10) He closed his eyes and asked God to speak to him. A cooling breeze blew across his skin. It felt as if God were whispering, "Yes, my child, I am here."*

Under what circumstances have you felt the presence of God most intensely?

List some ways you can "be still" and listen intently for God's direction.

Why is waiting an essential part of lining up our lives with God's will?

Chapter 11

If we say we have no sin, we deceive ourselves, and the truth is not in us. (1 John 1:8)

As you read through this chapter, what were you thinking and feeling about the Man?

What were you thinking and feeling about the Woman?

What stood out in your mind?

Excerpt: *Revealing weakness had always been hard for the Man.*

Why do you think it is so difficult to admit your weaknesses?

Think of a time you did admit a weakness to someone close to you. How did they respond?

Why do you think that revealing weakness is necessary if you desire to experience true intimacy with someone else?

Be completely honest with yourself and list some of your weaknesses.

How can admitting your weaknesses to God draw you closer to Him?

Excerpt: (In this chapter, the Man sat down and told his children—all of whom were 18 or older— the truth about what was going on in his life and how his life had gotten out of control.)

"I want you to be able to admit when you fail," the Man told his children, and I'm sorry if I've made it hard for you to say, "I messed up." We all mess up sometimes.

Caution: Before revealing such serious issues as this to your children, consider their need to know and whether they are mature enough to handle such knowledge.

Romans 3:10 says, "As it is written, 'There is none righteous, no, not one.'" How does this verse help you to realize that God knows we are imperfect yet loves us anyway?

Describe a time when someone overlooked one of your flaws and conveyed God's unconditional love to you.

How did it make you feel?

How could you begin to develop a climate of unconditional
love toward those you care most about?

Chapter 12

Do not remember the former things, or consider the things of old. I am about to do a new thing; now it springs forth, do you not perceive it? (Isaiah 43:18-19)

As you read through this chapter, what were you thinking and feeling about the Man?

What were you thinking and feeling about the Woman?

What stood out in your mind?

Excerpt: *Church had become an island of refuge for the Man and the Woman. Being around other Christians was a ready source of energy and inspiration. As a way to thank God for blessing them in so many ways—and as a way to turn their thoughts to something positive—they spent most of their free time doing volunteer work.*

Are you satisfied with your current level of involvement in reaching out to help others?

List some ways you could directly begin to serve others (not just donate money) through your church or local nonprofit organization.

Why is it so important to be acutely aware of the grace that God is extending to you during a time of adversity?

Excerpt: *The Woman often felt that their entire marriage had been a fraud, but the Man knew they had shared much genuine love. He recognized that his secret life had prevented them from having the kind of relationship that God intended, but he didn't believe it rendered everything else meaningless.*

List some ways sexual sin tears at the fabric of a relationship.

Do you believe that if one spouse sins against the other, it negates all the good that has occurred in the relationship? Why?

Excerpt: *The Man picked a letter from the stack of mail and opened it. The Workshop organizers were inviting him to an alumni weekend at the end of the month. They were also inviting alumni to share their stories with the men who would be attending the Workshop for the first time, men who would be where he had been fifteen months ago. He sensed that God was opening a door for him—but he was hesitant.*

Has God ever called you to do something you were not willing to do? If so, what was it?

Why do you think you were unwilling?

Chapter 13

Then the Lord put out his hand and touched my mouth; and the Lord said to me, "Now I have put my words in your mouth." (Jeremiah 1:9)

As you read through this chapter, what were you thinking and feeling about the Man?

What were you thinking and feeling about the Woman?

What stood out in your mind?

Excerpt: *The Man checked in at the hotel and went to his room. He took out the testimony he was going to deliver and read it out loud. He had to stop several times because he was overcome with emotion. He had asked God to direct his hand, and God had helped him bare his soul. As uncomfortable as he was about speaking before a large group, he was at peace knowing that this is what God had brought him here to do.*

Describe a risk that you have taken over the past few years.

What type of personal growth did you experience as a result of taking that risk?

Trusting that God equips those whom he calls, what kind of risk might you take to further God's purposes that would pull you out of your comfort zone?

Excerpt: *As soon as he got back to his room, the Man rejoiced in the miracle that God had performed. God had helped him put aside his fears to deliver a message of hope and repentance. God had used his pain and suffering for good.*

Have you ever experienced a season of adversity or witnessed someone else going through such a time where you saw God bring about positive results? Describe what happened.

What obstacles do you believe are standing in the way of your being fully obedient to the will of God for your life?

Chapter 14

When my soul was embittered, when I was pricked in heart, I was stupid and ignorant; I was like a brute beast toward you. (Psalm 73:21-22)

As you read through this chapter, what were you thinking and feeling about the Man?

What were you thinking and feeling about the Woman?

What stood out in your mind?

Excerpt: *It was late afternoon, and the hospital room was quiet. The Man sat at his father's bedside, watching him die. The doctors had given his father days, maybe a week. The Man felt nothing. He was emotionless in a moment that cried out for emotion.*

List the names of the people you have wronged in your life and what it was that you did to them.

What actions could you take today to mend those relationships?

If mending the relationship is not possible, what could you do to at least make peace with them?

If any of them are deceased, write a letter of apology.

Think of a time when you paid someone back for a wrong you believed he or she committed against you. What did you do and how did your actions affect the relationship?

Excerpt: (The Man is referring to a video he had watched with the Son the previous night.) *"It was a powerful message, you know, how God can forgive anything, even something as awful as aborting a child,"* the Man said to the Son. *"That would be a hard decision to make,"* the Son said. *"What do you think you'd do if that happened to you?"* Without thinking, the Man blurted out, *"That did happen to me."* His candor surprised him. Normally, he would have carefully considered whether he should reveal such a personal secret.

What are the risks involved in being totally honest with someone else?

What are the potential benefits?

On a scale of 1 to 10—with 1 being "very open" and 10 being "completely guarded"—how guarded do you think you are about your thoughts and feelings?

How does being emotionally guarded negatively affect a relationship?

Excerpt: *The Man had always demonstrated his love for his wife and children the way many men do—by providing for them, fixing things around the house, and performing other manly duties. These were legitimate expressions of love, but the Man now saw that they were not enough. He needed to display his love and affection outwardly.*

List some ways you communicate love to those you care about.

How effective do you think those efforts are?

Do you think that those persons would agree or disagree with your assessment?

What are some ways of expressing love that you could add to what you already do?

Chapter 15

Blessed is anyone who endures temptation. (James 1:12)

As you read through this chapter, what were you thinking and feeling about the Man?

What were you thinking and feeling about the Woman?

What stood out in your mind?

Excerpt: *The Man thought about how he had grown over the past year and a half.*

How have you grown emotionally in recent weeks?

How have you grown spiritually?

How have your significant relationships improved?

Excerpt: *If the Man had one regret, it was that he had not been honest with the Woman about his struggles with temptation. He felt he was in a Catch-22: If he admitted that he still wrestled with temptation, the Woman would fear that their situation was hopeless; if he insisted that he was never tempted, she would doubt him.*

Why is it important to be honest about your specific areas of sexual temptation?

What actions can you take to limit your exposure to sexual temptation? Be specific. For example: What places, TV shows, movies, magazines, Web sites, etc., should you avoid because they might be sources of temptation?

Are there people in your life who may be causing you to compromise your values, negatively influence the way you think about sex and sexuality, and lead you into situations that should be out of bounds? Examples: A co-worker suggests having lunch at a restaurant that features provocatively dressed females. A friend periodically sends you emails that contain graphic sexual images. If so, how can you politely but firmly communicate to them that certain activities are not appropriate for you?

In addition to being diligent about avoiding temptation, what steps can you take to nourish your mind with God's word?

At the end of this chapter, the Man wrote down three things:

Temptation is inevitable.
Even Jesus was tempted.
Temptation is not sin.

How can accepting that temptation is inevitable ease the frustration you might feel when temptation occurs in your life, even though you did your best to avoid it?

Why should knowing that Jesus was tempted give you comfort?

Why is it important to understand that temptation is not sin?

Chapter 16

For if they fall, one will lift up the other; but woe to one who is alone and falls and does not have another to help. (Ecclesiastes 4:9-10)

As you read through this chapter, what were you thinking and feeling about the Man?

What were you thinking and feeling about the Woman?

What stood out in your mind?

Excerpt: *Soon after the dust from the move had settled, the Man and the Woman began to argue about the same things. The Man had wanted to believe that he and the Woman were finished with the hurt and mistrust, but they were not.*

Why must you be on guard when you begin to feel that you have done enough and start walking away from the commitments you have made?

How can these prideful feelings create a climate of fear and mistrust?

Revisit the commitments to change that you have made.

Which ones are you still honoring?

List any commitments you need to renew.

Why is it important to accept that healing is a process that will take time?

Excerpt: *Because the Man was farther along in recovery, he looked forward to helping his Accountability Partner avoid some of the mistakes he had made. It felt good to talk to someone who didn't judge him. He had missed his conversations with the Pastor and the Therapist, but he had been reluctant to tell his story to anyone else.*

Have you considered how being open about your own journey could help others who are facing a similar challenge? (To connect with such people, visit www.theshadowchristian. com.)

Excerpt: *The Man and the Woman decided to begin praying together every morning and separately for each other, and they read the Bible each night before they went to sleep.*

How is praying with and for someone you love a powerful way to build intimacy?

If you are not currently doing so, what is keeping you from taking that step?

List your top five priorities in order of importance.

1)
2)
3)
4)
5)

Is the way you spend your time and money consistent with the priorities you just listed?

What changes might be necessary to better live out those priorities?

Excerpt: *"Why does she need to know my every move?" the Man had asked the Therapist. "This is all about trust," the Therapist had replied. "The way to build trust is by being accountable—being where you are supposed to be, doing what you are supposed to be doing. Over time, the Woman will grow to be more secure about trusting you."*

The above sentiment can be expressed with this simple formula:

$$\frac{Commitment + Consistency}{Time} = Trust\ Regained$$

Why is honoring your commitments over time the best way to reassure someone and rebuild trust?

Chapter 17

Bear with one another and, if anyone has a complaint against another, forgive each other; just as the Lord has forgiven you, you also must forgive. (Colossians 3:13)

As you read through this chapter, what were you thinking and feeling about the Man?

What were you thinking and feeling about the Woman?

What stood out in your mind?

Excerpt: *"If we don't forgive those who have sinned against us,"* the Pastor said, *"we will remain a prisoner of the sin."*

Holding on to unforgiveness can give you a false sense of control over the one who sinned against you. But the reality is that unforgiveness burdens your own soul. When you forgive, you unlock the door to the prison you have created for yourself. List the people in your life who have hurt you that you need to forgive.

List the people in your life who you have hurt and need to ask to forgive you.

Excerpt: *The Woman invited the Man out into the back yard and handed him a homemade greeting card. The Man opened it and read her words: "I know I've said I didn't need to say the words 'I forgive you,' because of the love I've shown you. But I was wrong. As of this day, I forgive you."*

Why do you think it is so hard to say, "I was wrong"?

Write down the most unkind or selfish thing you did this past week to someone you care about.

Now go apologize and ask him/her to forgive you. Don't just say, "I'm sorry." You must ask, "Will you forgive me?"

How can regularly admitting wrongs and asking the one you wronged to forgive you cultivate a habit of forgiveness?

Excerpt: *The Man thanked God for answering his prayer. The Woman's inability to forgive had kept her trapped in a cycle of anger and resentment. Now she was free.*

As much as you would like to, you cannot undo the past. But the past can steal your future if you let it. How can unforgiveness prevent you from letting go of the past and moving forward?

Chapter 18

So if anyone is in Christ, there is a new creation; everything old has passed away; see, everything has become new. (2 Corinthians 5:17)

As you read through this chapter, what were you thinking and feeling about the Man?

What were you thinking and feeling about the Woman?

What stood out in your mind?

Excerpt: *The Man thought about how radiant the Woman had been last night and how affectionately she had looked at him, a look of love he thought he'd never see again. He offered a silent prayer of gratitude. "Thank you, Lord, for the gift of the Woman."*

Why do you think it is so easy to take the ones we love for granted?

What are you willing to do to restore the relationships that matter most to you?

Excerpt: *The Man and the Woman talked more openly about what it meant to have the kind of healthy physical relationship with each other that God intended.*

When it comes to sex, what do you believe is appropriate behavior?

What is your understanding of God's design for sex?

The Bible says that God intended sex to be a mind, body, and spirit connection between a husband and wife. Have you ever experienced that degree of connection with your spouse?

Why does God's design for sex, as an expression of love between a husband and wife, provide the greatest degree of fulfillment?

At the end of this chapter, the Man lists ten things "real men" do.

Real men tell the truth.
Real men admit their mistakes.
Real men are not ruled by their desires.
Real men respect their wives' boundaries.

Real men are spiritual leaders at home.
Real men help their wives blossom.
Real men give more than they take.
Real men aren't afraid to cry.
Real men are joyful.
Real men need God.

Circle the ones you feel you do well.

List the ones you feel you still need to work on.

Chapter 19

But I am like a green olive tree in the house of God. I trust in the steadfast love of God forever and ever. (Psalm 52:8)

As you read through this chapter, what were you thinking and feeling about the Man?

What were you thinking and feeling about the Woman?

What stood out in your mind?

Excerpt: *The Man often had doubts and fears, but when he did, he knew where to turn. He remembered that whenever he relied on his own understanding, he stumbled.*

Where do you tend to turn when you have doubts and fears?

How often do you lean on your own understanding?

Excerpt: *The Man and the Woman could feel God more intensely in their lives.*

Scripture says we are to "pray without ceasing," if we want to feel God's presence more intensely. How can you begin to develop the habit of connecting with God throughout the day for guidance and comfort?

Think of someone you love. When have you felt closest to that person?

Why do you think you felt so close to them then?

The final chapter ends with these words: *They both knew they had to share what God had done for them.*

God calls each of us to share with others how His grace has transformed our lives. God will let you know when it's time for you to tell your story.

Will you choose to obey Him when he does?

7 Simple Ways to Help Your Wife

1) Control your anger. Even though it may be a response to the frustration you are feeling, she will interpret anger as an indication that you have something to hide.

2) Be patient. Healing and rebuilding trust will take time—lots of time.

3) Renew your commitment regularly. It will remind her of the changes you've made, and it will help to reassure her.

4) Be honest. Tell her the truth about your struggle with temptation—and about everything else. There can be no true intimacy without honesty.

5) Pray with her. There is no greater way for a husband and wife to grow closer than to share their connection with God.

6) Pray for her. Ask God to heal her wounds and calm her fears. Praying for your wife regularly is another way to express unselfish love.

7) Smile more.

7 Simple Ways to Help Your Husband

1) Do not tolerate sexual sin. Your husband's soul and your self-respect are at stake.

2) Do not forgive too quickly. Wait for God's perfect timing.

3) Insist that he honor his commitments. He must demonstrate over the long haul that he can be trusted.

4) Accept that temptation is not sin. Know that each time he avoids temptation he is becoming a better man.

5) Accept that recovery is something you both must live with and manage.

6) Pray with him. Connecting with God will bring you closer.

7) Pray for him. Ask God to give him the strength to be the man he was created to be.

To contact Al or Linda or to order copies of *The Shadow Christian,* visit: TheShadowChristian.com